KNOWLEDGE MANAGEMENT AND RISK STRATEGIES

Akira Ishikawa

Emeritus Professor, Aoyama Gakuin University, Japan

Isamu Naka

Finance & IT Consultant, Hitachi, Japan

KNOWLEDGE MANAGEMENT AND RISK STRATEGIES

World Scientific

NEW JERSEY · LONDON · SINGAPORE · BEIJING · SHANGHAI · HONG KONG · TAIPEI · CHENNAI

Published by

World Scientific Publishing Co. Pte. Ltd.

5 Toh Tuck Link, Singapore 596224

USA office: 27 Warren Street, Suite 401-402, Hackensack, NJ 07601

UK office: 57 Shelton Street, Covent Garden, London WC2H 9HE

Library of Congress Cataloging-in-Publication Data
Ishikawa, Akira, 1934–
    Knowledge management and risk strategies / by Akira Ishikawa & Isamu Naka.
    p. cm.
    Includes bibliographical references and index.
    ISBN-13 978-981-256-890-8 -- ISBN-10 981-256-890-5
        1. Knowledge management. 2. Information technology--Management.
    3. Risk management. I. Naka, Isamu. II. Title.

    HD30.2.I84 2007
    658.4'038--dc22

                                                                2006050091

British Library Cataloguing-in-Publication Data
A catalogue record for this book is available from the British Library.

Typeset by Stallion Press
Email: enquiries@stallionpress.com

Printed in Singapore by World Scientific Printers (S) Pte Ltd

Prologue

The Era of Knowledge Selection

1) The Current Situation of Employment and Work-Sharing in Japan

Japan's unemployment rate hit a record high of 5.5% in January 2003. With the economy being stagnant, work-sharing has been much discussed in recent years. Work-sharing is a scheme to retain the workforce by reducing the workload of each employee, and has already been introduced in European countries, such as Germany, the Netherlands, and France. The Ministry of Health, Labor and Welfare released a report on work-sharing in April 2001.[1] It classified four types of work-sharing: Emergency Measure Type, Diversified Working Patterns Type, Measure Aimed at Middle-Aged and Elderly Workers Type, and Job Creation Type.[2] Several electrical manufacturers and local governments have introduced work-sharing schemes, most of which are Emergency Type, to survive the severe economic recession.

---

[1] Mitsui Knowledge Industry, Research Institute, commissioned by the then Ministry of Labor, "Survey Report on Work-Sharing," April 2001.

[2] Different types of work-sharing are classified according to their purposes. Emergency Measure Type is an emergency measure to retain trained employees. Diversified Working Patterns Type is to create more job opportunities, especially for older employees and women, by introducing diversified working patterns (i.e., shorter and more flexible working hours). Measure Aimed at Middle-Aged and Elderly Workers Type purports to secure jobs for older employees. Job Creation Type is work-sharing for general employees.

The problem with work-sharing is that management tends to consider work-sharing as a means of payroll reduction, while it is a way to secure jobs for employees. Therefore, management and unions often disagree when it comes to the ideal employment system, although they can manage to come to an agreement on a work-sharing scheme as an emergency measure. They simply have different views of the new society, where work-sharing is a mode of business.

Apart from the unemployment crisis caused by the lingering recession, there is another reason why work-sharing has been much debated in Japan. The change in the environment, caused by what is called "globalization", made obsolete the conventional Japanese employment system, its ethics and values.

2)   The Dawn of a New Era

What is the change in the environment surrounding Japan? Let us first examine it in the development of digital and network technologies, then in the change in the lifespan of knowledge.

The development of digital and network technology

The rapid developments in the IT industry have prompted the globalization of economies, overthrowing both the industrial structure and the traditional consumers' view of "shopping".

It is now possible to communicate easily with people in remote places as long as you are connected to networks. Also, the new distribution channel called "E-commerce" makes it possible to do business with customers from all over the world, even without having physical premises.

Furthermore, XML web service technology, which has recently been introduced, has facilitated communication between independent information processing services.[3] With XML, it is possible for

---

[3] XML (extensible markup language) is a simple and universal format to publish and exchange structured documents and data. It is derived from SGML.

a company to provide only that part of the information processing service that they are strong at, and to use the IPS of other providers for the rest. Thus, companies can offer services highly sustained in total. Companies no longer need to provide all the information processing equipment necessary for their business.

All this has caused drastic changes in the business world. What used to be important factors in business transactions, such as geographic advantages, connections and local business conventions, are now outshone by the fundamental value in offers themselves. Companies will have to focus on differentiating their offers in terms of quality and value. The developments in the IT industry have brought about a paradigm shift in corporate competency: the focus has shifted from long-term, stable business relations to products and services that exactly satisfy customers' demands.

Shortened lifespan of knowledge

It takes various forms of knowledge, e.g., design engineering, processing technology, product design and production know-how, to deliver products and services. Knowledge, which forms the base of products and services, however, has been becoming increasingly short-lived in recent years.[4] Before 1959, a piece of knowledge was profitable for 21.8 years; since 1990, it is only profitable for 3.2 years. This shows that knowledge is no longer so valuable as stock.

The decrease in the shelf life of knowledge, combined with the rapid developments in IT technologies, necessitates that products and services meet the customers' demands exactly. At the same time, these two phenomena are nullifying the value of knowledge as stock. Companies will have to carefully select the knowledge necessary to deliver products and services that meet precise customer demands. What is the consequence of this for the business world?

---

[4]National Institute of Science and Technology Policy, "Assessment of the Effects of R&D Policy on Economic Growth," June 1999, pp. 26, 28 and 30.

Knowledge selection is not an easy matter. Knowledge is a comprehensive word; patents and copyright, for example, may be called knowledge, but an employee's experience can also be called knowledge. Take a consulting firm, for example: aside from their expertise, "how to get through a sticky patch" or "how to get a customer interested" can also be deemed important knowledge, which only those who have gained it through experience have access to. This demonstrates the intangible and invisible nature of knowledge — hence, knowledge needs practitioners. Knowledge lies in the memory of the person who has practiced it. Unlike objects, knowledge cannot be passed on from A to B in a business deal. Knowledge management is intimately connected with personnel management, especially in its transfer. Therefore, facilitated knowledge selection and the shortened storage life of knowledge will gravely affect lifetime employment and seniority-based pay systems, which have been the symbol of the relationship between companies and employees in Japan.

In the struggle to rebuild the nation's devastated economy after World War II, Japan had only to realize knowledge transfer by copying the successful examples of business models in the USA and Europe. Furthermore, as the government adopted a complete industrial targeting policy, Japanese corporations were allowed to focus on enlarging their market shares and developing new technology. Luckily, the Japanese economy prospered, so there was always high demand for manpower. Also, an employee was able to mature in the same company that he joined after graduating from college, accumulating experience and knowledge. Therefore, the seniority-based pay system worked quite well in Japan. The shortening of the knowledge lifespan, however, undermines these premises. Unlike in the past, employees nowadays will not be able to train and gain new knowledge in their jobs and build up their careers throughout their entire working years in a single company. This is because though companies cannot afford to train all their employees by themselves any more, they still need to have employees with the necessary expertise to take advantage of business opportunities.

How to manage knowledge selection, including personnel management, will be the key to survival for companies, when corporate competency shifts from stable business contacts to the quality of their offers, and when the value of knowledge, which is the foundation of products and services, is becoming more and more short-lived.

As will be seen in Part 2, Chapter 4, work-sharing can be an effective way to operate knowledge selection smoothly. Work-sharing questions the conventional balance of responsibility between management and employees, as well as the value systems that have formed the employment system in Japan (such as lifetime employment), and heightens our awareness of "career lifespan".

In the following chapters, we will focus on knowledge transfer, and discuss the effect of knowledge selection on companies and employees in an organization "that attempts to gain benefits from knowledge". Knowledge transfer and the benefits from knowledge have previously been considered uncertain, and knowledge selection risk has not been given much attention. The shortening of knowledge value lifespan will change all that. It will also have a profound impact on companies' employment policies and employees' strategies for gaining knowledge. We will then discuss the social basis, such as work-sharing and the personnel supply derivative business, in order to deal with knowledge selection risk.

The structure of this book is as follows:

Part 1: The End of Knowledge Stock and the Emerging Knowledge Selection Risk.

In Part 1, the changing environment will be discussed, with the focus on knowledge.

In Chapters 1 and 2, we will delineate the definition of knowledge in various fields, and come to a comprehensive definition of knowledge. We will also demonstrate that in order to keep utilizing knowledge in a society, we need a system to train and maintain practitioners of knowledge, which will cost money and time to establish.

In Chapter 3, we will show that there is a lifespan for the value of knowledge, which has been shortening in recent years. It will be discussed that this shortening of knowledge lifespan will force selection of knowledge on companies and employees, and that this selection will involve risk: the risk of not being able to gain new knowledge, or of not being able to gain the expected benefit even if that knowledge is successfully gained.

In Chapter 4, it will be discussed that when knowledge lifespan is shortening, companies will find it difficult to maintain a lifetime employment system and to support various costs pertaining to knowledge selection. Also, controlling knowledge selection risk will be crucial, since employees will have to select knowledge by themselves.

Part 2: How to Manage Knowledge Selection Risk.

In Part 2, the infrastructures necessary to manage knowledge selection risk and ways to adjust the exposure to risk by the entire society will be discussed.

In Chapter 1, we will point to problems that society will have to face as knowledge selection risk manifests itself.

From Chapters 2 to 5, we will introduce specific examples of how to induce knowledge to become visible, how to match-make knowledge demand, how to secure the time that knowledge transfer takes, and how to enhance the efficiency of knowledge transfer. On the basis of such ingredients, it is possible for us to depict the framework of knowledge selection society (Chapter 6), as shown in Figure 26.

In the Epilogue, we will present the summary.

About the Authors

Akira Ishikawa

Professor Emeritus and former Dean, Graduate School of International Politics, Economics and Business, Aoyama Gakuin University. Studied at the University of Washington and University of Texas, Graduate School of Business Administration, with post-doctoral studies at Massachusetts Institute of Technology. Served as a lecturer at University of Texas, as an assistant professor at the Graduate School of New York University, and as a professor at the Graduate School of Rutgers University. Authored *Strategic Budgeting, Future Computer and Information Systems, Corporate Planning and Control Model Systems*, and others. Coauthored *The Kyoto Model: The Challenge of Japanese Management Strategy Meeting Global Standards, The Success of 7-Eleven Japan, Top Global Companies in Japan*, and others. Translated *Managing Chaos, Defense Management*, and others.

Isamu Naka

Finance and IT consultant, Hitachi Consulting, Hitachi. Chartered Member of The Security Analysts Association of Japan. Studied at Tokyo University of Science, and at Graduate School of International Politics, Economics, and Business, Aoyama Gakuin University. Ph.D. candidate, Japan Advanced Institute of Science and Technology (JAIST).

Contents

Part 1

THE END OF KNOWLEDGE STOCK AND THE EMERGING KNOWLEDGE SELECTION RISK

The importance of intellectual property management has long been understood. Knowledge, however, has become increasingly short-lived; there is a danger that the knowledge a corporation has accumulated over a period of time may instantly become an unprofitable asset. Therefore, it has become essential for corporate competency to select the right knowledge.

From the employees' point of view, the shortened lifespan of knowledge threatens the system of lifetime employment. They have to take "lifespan of career" into account when deciding on their career paths.

Chapter 1

The Shift in the Definition of "Knowledge"

There have been studies on knowledge in a variety of disciplines, such as engineering, management and psychology. The domain of the term "knowledge" has seen a considerable change and expansion, even if we look only at recent years. We will delineate the transition of "knowledge" in each discipline and seek a comprehensive definition of "knowledge" for this book.

1.1 The Range of "Knowledge"

1) *The range of "knowledge" in engineering*

The field of engineering that deals with the systematization of knowledge is called knowledge engineering, which originated with the Heuristic Programming Project (HPP) at Stanford University in 1965. The HPP succeeded in completing an expert system to deduct the structural formulas of organic compounds: DENDRAL. This opened up the possibility of computer systems solving problems in place of human experts, by transplanting expert knowledge onto computers. Since then, researchers vigorously constructed various expert systems, such as MYCIN.[1] These systems, however, could only manage knowledge that could be stated in the "rule" formula — if A, then B — which limited their problem-solving ability. Nonetheless,

---

[1] MYCIN is a medical expert system, which gives advice on treatment for blood infections and meningitis. It was developed at Stanford University in 1972.

this triggered the study of knowledge engineering, since in building expert systems, the idea was promoted that the representation of knowledge should be approached as an object of scientific study, rather than as a series of randomly derived rules.

The objectives of knowledge engineering are to grasp knowledge systematically and to utilize it effectively. The main task is to codify knowledge in a form that can be integrated into computer systems. In other words, the "knowledge" in knowledge engineering is "that which can be stored and sorted in a way that can be readily accessed when needed".[2]

2)   *The range of "knowledge" in psychology*

What "knowledge" means in psychology varies greatly, depending on which branch you turn to.

In behavioral psychology, knowledge is considered to be a mass of "stimuli–response" relationships, since its main focus is on analyzing the rules of those relationships. Pavlov's well-known experiments in conditioned reflexes are the prime examples of this school.[3]

The information processing approach in cognitive psychology conceives human intellect as an information processing system, and it aims to comprehend mental processes by identifying this system. This approach classifies memory into three categories, according to the duration of memory retention: sensory memory, short-term memory and long-term memory. Knowledge is defined as what is stored in the long-term memory. This school of thought, however, began to decline in the late 1970s, as it became obvious that it was too simple to fully elucidate the mechanism of human cognition.

---

[2]The original quote is from Information Processing Society of Japan (Ed.), *Knowledge Engineering*, Ohmsha, 1987, p. 4.
[3]Ivan Petrovich Pavlov (1849–1936) was a Russian physiologist, psychologist and physician. While measuring dogs' saliva in his experiments, Pavlov discovered the phenomenon of "conditioned responses".

The Piagetian school in the theory of cognitive development defines that knowledge is actively constructed.[4] It assumes that men have cognitive structures, and that knowledge is constructed through adaptations of cognitive structures to the environment.[5]

3) *The range of "knowledge" in management theories*

Mottoes such as "knowledge is a competitive asset" or "how you manage knowledge decides corporate competitiveness" have long been heard in the business world. It can safely be said that the term "knowledge management" has entered the lexicon of management studies. However, yet again, what "knowledge" means here is not a simple matter.

The management guru, Peter F. Drucker, explains the shift in the definition of the word "knowledge". He says that knowledge, which used to apply to "being", came to be applied to "doing", such as "tools, processes and products", and ultimately to "knowledge" itself.[6] That is, the nature of knowledge changed from the abstract and existential (e.g., "why the world exists") to the concrete and practical (e.g., "how to produce plastic").

Ikujiro Nonaka, a specialist on corporate creativity, refers to two types of knowledge: explicit and tacit knowledge.[7] Explicit knowledge can be transmitted between individuals systematically or formally, whereas tacit knowledge is difficult to formalize or share with others as it is personal and circumstantial.[8] This notion of "tacit knowledge" was groundbreaking, as it broadened the concept of

---

[4]Jean Piaget (1896–1980) was a Swiss philosopher and psychologist. He developed new fields of science, namely developmental psychology and genetic epistemology.

[5]Cognitive structures are mental schemes that help us make sense of the environment, and they determine our behavior and responses.

[6]The original text that the author refers to here is Drucker, P. F., *Post-Capitalist Society*, Collins, 1994.

[7]Nonaka, Ikujiro and Hirotaka Takeuchi, *The Knowledge-Creating Company*, Toyo Keizai, 1996.

[8]Examples of explicit knowledge are data, scientific formulas and manuals. Examples of tacit knowledge include craft skills, personal beliefs and values.

"knowledge" from codified information to include even inarticulate mental muddle. Nonaka believes that new knowledge is created through social interactions of the two kinds of knowledge.

In recent years, many management consulting firms have started to introduce "knowledge management" as one of their business strategies. What knowledge management refers to is quite extensive though — it varies from the construction and management of a knowledge base as seen in knowledge engineering, to that of a "platform" for information as an auxiliary knowledge creation tool.

In addition to formally or systematically codified knowledge, some consultants include in knowledge those intangible concepts, such as brand names that evoke certain feelings among consumers, or even a specific atmosphere created among a group of people (see Table 1).

Thus, the domain of "knowledge" differs according to disciplines, and it has been expanding in each discipline as the study has progressed, generally from what can be systematically and logically studied to what is difficult to articulate, such as "atmosphere".

Table 1:   Examples of Knowledge as Property

	Empirical Knowledge	Formalized Knowledge	Institutional Knowledge
Market Knowledge	◇ Knowledge of consumers, learned from experience with products and services ◇ Knowledge of distribution networks, learned from experience with products and services	◇ Assessment of brand equity corporations	◇ Knowledge gained from networking and communicating with customers (e.g., consumer monitoring) ◇ Knowledge concerning market and customers, gained from distribution networks

Table 1: (*Continued*)

	Empirical Knowledge	Formalized Knowledge	Institutional Knowledge
Organizational Knowledge	◇ Knowledge and abilities that employees have obtained ◇ Core knowledge and abilities of specific professions	◇ Knowledge and abilities concerning development, planning, design of products ◇ Quality perception	◇ Systems for organizational training (educational programs and training know-how) ◇ Knowledge circulated in an organization via communication systems (e.g., contents of e-mail)
Product-Based Knowledge	◇ Know-how for products and services that can be shared ◇ Traditional skilled knowledge, such as methods of manufacturing	◇ Product concepts (quality and quantity of concepts of products both in the market and in development) ◇ Product design, including models and prototypes	◇ Complementary and specific knowledge of products, such as how to use products (partly formalized by manuals) ◇ Social and legal knowledge application system of products (environmental issues, product liability)

Source: Konno, Noboru, *Management of Intellectual Property*, Nihon Keizai Shimbun, 1998.

1.2 The Basic Nature of "Knowledge"

It is only natural that "knowledge" studied in various disciplines has different meanings, as different fields of study have different objectives. However, there is one characteristic of knowledge that is common to all. That is, knowledge is valuable only when there are

Figure 1:   Historic Sanctuary of Machu Picchu (Inca Civilization)

people to appreciate it. However advanced a technology is, it dies with the individual who owns the knowledge, unless it is communicated to another.

The Maya and Inca people of Central America left proof of their highly advanced civilizations in the ruins of their ancient cities (see Figure 1). Yet it is impossible for us to decipher their civilizations minutely, as the records of their culture, including their technologies and philosophies, are mostly lost.

Hence, we define "knowledge" in this book as "that which is lost unless deliberately maintained", including tacit knowledge such as craftsmanship. This means that besides what we have seen above, "knowledge" includes folklore, music and cultural tendencies. We call it knowledge if it is given a name and can be passed on to others.

The Cost of Knowledge Transfer and the Motives Behind Knowledge Inheritance

When knowledge is defined as "that which is lost unless deliberately maintained", it becomes clear that we need some kind of system to maintain and transfer knowledge. In this chapter, we will argue that knowledge transfer involves more than mere payment for patent rights, for example. Training the people who are to practice that particular knowledge is essential. We will also discuss that sometimes people decide to pass on certain knowledge with quite arbitrary intentions.

2.1 Knowledge Transfer System

"Knowledge transfer" means the passing on of knowledge among individuals and groups. There have been various systems and measures of knowledge transfer in Japan.

Among social systems of knowledge transfer, there are two types: in type 1, students are gathered in one place (e.g., schools and training institutes); in type 2, instructors and students share the same experience (e.g., the apprentice system). The former system is often used to transfer formalized thoughts and perspectives, whereas the latter is used to transfer implicit ones.

There are a variety of ways to transfer knowledge: the learner might simply read a book, participate in a class or a seminar, use multimedia learning materials, or learn mainly from questions and answers as in case study classes. Nowadays, flexible courses that allow students to fit them into their schedules (e.g., correspondence courses and e-learning) are gaining popularity.

Students sometimes take examinations after completing a course to see if they have successfully learned the knowledge or not. These examinations may have strict criteria, or may be assessed qualitatively by instructors. If they pass the examinations, the students are considered capable of practising the particular knowledge that they have learned.

It can be safely said that "instruction" is necessary for knowledge transfer of any kind. Instructors might directly teach learners, or they might write books, thus teaching learners indirectly.

In our society, knowledge transfer has been conducted by combinations of various types of instruction, both implicit and explicit, such as textbooks, programs by educational establishments, or examinations.

- Knowledge in compulsory education is passed on by such media as textbooks from publishers, auxiliary teaching materials, programs and examinations by elementary and junior high schools, private tutoring schools, correspondence courses, e-learning, and finally, by daily communication with parents.
- There are various examinations for essential knowledge in the IT industry. For example, the Information Technology Engineers Examination (ITEE) is a knowledge transfer system with various types of instructions: textbooks and auxiliary teaching materials from publishers, training schools, correspondence courses, e-learning courses, and mock exams.[1]
- Techniques and perspectives crucial for trades are often learned in on-the-job training. The target knowledge for craftsmen in metalworking and pottery, for example, is not usually compatible with explicit instruction like textbooks. Instead, trainees learn

---

[1]The Information Technology Engineers Examination (ITEE) was first administered in 1969, and in 1970, became a national examination under the then Ministry of International Trade & Industry (MITI), now Ministry of Economy, Trade & Industry (METI). From http://www.jitec.jp/index-e.html

from repeating basic techniques in on-the-job training, or from sharing experiences with craftsmen in an apprentice system.

A survey on the career development of office workers reports that on-the-job training (OJT) has become the main method of employee training in corporations: 53.3% conduct in-house training by OJT, while 43.3% by the combination of OJT and off-the-job-training.[2]

It might seem risky to assign jobs to employees who do not have the appropriate knowledge for the task yet, but OJT is a valid method of instruction, just another type of "instruction" for knowledge transfer in companies.

Hereafter, various kinds of instructions for transferring a certain piece of knowledge will be collectively called the "Knowledge Transfer System" of that particular knowledge. For example, instructions for bookkeeping, such as study guides, teachers, schools and companies, are collectively called "knowledge transfer system for bookkeeping knowledge".

2.2   Two Costs of Knowledge Transfer Systems

Knowledge does not do anything if it merely exists in a book or in someone's mind. Knowledge is valuable only when it is understood and practiced in a human society, granting people economic profit or emotional pleasure. If knowledge is buried in books, it will only become obsolete one day, and it is useless if it is only stored in a person's mind, excellent though their mind may be, as it will only disappear when they die.

To maintain and pass on knowledge, we need to operate a knowledge transfer system, for which we have to incur a certain cost.

When a person with a special knowledge writes a textbook, works as a teacher, or holds examinations for learners, there is a cost involved. At the same time, learners will have to spend time on

---

[2]Study Committee on the Japanese Employment System, "Research on the Condition of Workers' Career Development and Awareness," June–August 1999.

Table 2:   Knowledge Transfer Costs

Types of Costs	Content
Operational (fiscal) Cost	Cost to run a Knowledge Transfer System
Time Cost	Cost for learners to receive support for Knowledge Transfer System, and to understand knowledge

reading textbooks, going to schools, and sitting for exams, though they may or may not successfully gain knowledge.

From the learners' point of view, the former is the fiscal cost of receiving education, i.e., it is the operational cost of that particular knowledge transfer system. The latter is time cost: the time spent to gain knowledge. To run a knowledge transfer system, both operational (fiscal) and time cost have to be defrayed (see Table 2).

2.3   Examples of Knowledge Transfer Cost

We will examine several examples of actual knowledge transfer costs, arguing that if the costs are not covered properly, it will have a negative influence on the success of the inheritance of the knowledge.

1)   *Cost of compulsory education*

The compulsory education system in Japan has been in operation since the early 20th century, with revisions to the syllabuses made according to changes in society's needs. Textbooks are edited to respond to changes in society, and though it has been highly controversial, there is a textbook appraisal society to examine the contents.[3] There is yet another layer in the textbook production mechanism: each education board selects official textbooks. It can be safely said

---

[3]Dissatisfied with the official history textbooks, a group with right-wing tendencies called the Japanese Society for History Textbook Reform was formed to publish their own "new history textbooks", which have been highly controversial in Japan, Korea and China.

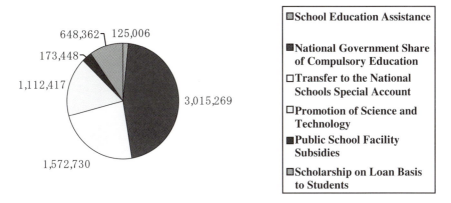

Figure 2:   Education and Science Budget FY 2001 (million Yen)

that the knowledge transfer system to operate compulsory education has been firmly established in Japan.

According to the Japanese government's budget report in 2001, the Education and Science budget stands at 8% of the general account budget, reaching 6647.2 billion JPY, which was the largest expenditure next to Social Security Related and Public Work Related Expenditures, apart from National Debt Service and Local Allocation Tax Grants. Figure 2 shows the breakdown of the Education and Science budget.[4]

In Figure 2, the National Treasury's share of compulsory education expenses is shown, where the government supports half the wages of all the teachers in national and public elementary and junior high schools in Japan. The rest is incurred by the local governments. The entire personnel cost of education for the national government and the prefectural and municipal governments amounts to approximately 6.3 trillion JPY, with more than 700,000 teachers in all of Japan. The budget for the free distribution of textbooks program amounts to 44.1 billion JPY. The cost of the compulsory education system in Japan is over six trillion JPY, covering personnel and textbook costs alone.

---

[4]Figure 2 is from Ministry of Finance, "Summary of Budget and Fiscal Investment and Loan Program Plan, FY 2001," 2001.

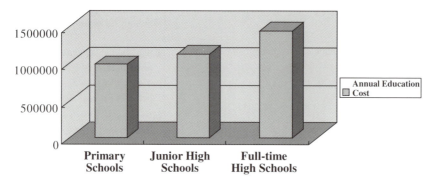

Figure 3:   Annual Education Cost per Student

Now we will examine the cost per student. Figure 3 shows the annual educational cost per student in 1998.[5] The educational cost per elementary school student is 980,913 JPY, and per junior high school student, 1,119,888 JPY. What should not be forgotten here is that apart from these fiscal costs, there is a time cost of nine years for compulsory education in Japan.

2)   *Training investment in companies*

When we look into training investment among major corporations, employee training programs held by the personnel development division of corporate headquarters in 2000 totaled on average 1.6 days of training per person. This translates into a direct training cost of 46,700 JPY, and an opportunity cost during the training period of 37,700 JPY, totaling 84,400 JPY per person.[6]

According to research concerning OJT in the information and communication technology industry by The Japan Institute for Labor Policy and Training, companies that hold OFF-JT programs stand at 49% (elementary SE), 42% (advanced SE), approximately

---

[5] Figure 3 is from *Japan Almanac 2002*, Asahi Shimbun, 2001.
[6] Personnel and Labor Management Study Group, "Research on Personnel Management and Training Investment in the Performance-Based Pay Era," 8 August 2000.

Table 3: Length of Training Courses in Corporations by Occupation (%)

	1–2 Days	3–5 Days	About 1 Week	2–3 Weeks	More than 1 Month	No Answer
Elementary SE	9.9	26.2	27.3	18.2	15.5	2.9
Advanced SE	10.5	30.4	34.4	16.6	5.9	2.6
Project Manager	14.5	35.0	30.2	14.0	4.1	2.6
Network Engineer	7.6	30.6	31.1	18.8	8.1	3.9

30% (project manager), and approximately 27% (network engineer). Table 3 shows length of training by size of firm.[7]

As we can see, training for project managers is three to five days, and for systems engineers, about a week. The cost of these training courses involves personnel costs relative to the number of training days, in addition to the direct training costs. Companies shoulder the necessary costs of training employees, who are essential to their business.

3) *Qualification costs*

There are a myriad of qualifications and accreditations in a variety of fields: law, accountancy, languages, and computer technologies. Among them are qualifications granted by the Japanese government (e.g., lawyer and accountant), qualifications of a semipublic nature (e.g., TOEIC), and qualifications granted by private companies (e.g., MCP, Microsoft Certified Professional). All of these qualifications require relative knowledge transfer, which naturally involves costs.

Table 4 is a summary of the required study time and course fees, taken from leaflets of courses for qualifications offered by several educational institutes.[8]

---

[7] Japan Research Institute of Labor, "FY 2001 White Paper," 2001, p. 147.
[8] From leaflets of various educational and training courses and software.

Table 4:   Average Time and Fees of Training Courses

Types of Qualifications	Average Study Time	Fees (JPY)
Financial Planner AFP	180	168,000
Certified Social Insurance Labour Consultant	350–680	241,500
Real Estate Transaction Manager	200	92,400
Administrative Notary	300	157,000
General/Domestic Travel Business Manager	200	65,000
Registered Customs Specialist	280	168,000
Care Manager	200	126,000

In the example of a real-estate broker course, it involves an average time cost of 200 h, and the operational cost of this knowledge transfer system is 120,000 to 200,000 JPY per person. Needless to say, the average time and fees of courses differs from institution to institution, and the actual hours needed to acquire qualifications differ among individual learners. Some might gain qualifications by merely studying books in a short time. Even so, there are time costs involved in the production of these books, and in the study of them. It is impossible to manage the transfer of knowledge necessary for qualifications without the fiscal and time costs being thoroughly covered.

No matter what kind of knowledge it is, it requires some kind of instruction to transmit it from one group to another. The two types of costs signify that the transaction of knowledge transfer is not complete with the payment of technical fees or patent royalty, but is only complete when the costs to turn a learner into a practitioner are entirely absorbed. Knowledge transfer is not only about monetary payment but also about constructing and managing the mechanism to train practitioners.

4)   *The relationship between knowledge transfer costs and knowledge inheritance*

We will examine several examples of how knowledge inheritance is affected, if the knowledge transfer costs are not fully paid.

Since the accident at Three Mile Island in 1979, no nuclear power stations have been built in the USA.[9] Nuclear reactors, such as those by General Electric Company (GE), have only been built in a few places, for example in Japan and Taiwan. On the back of lobbying by power plant officials and with a change of administration in the USA, the Nuclear Energy Institute announced their plan of building a number of new nuclear power stations in May 2001.

This exchange in the hearings before the US House of Representatives on 27 June 2001 is quite interesting. Billy Tauzin, a Republican, asked Richard A. Meserve, Chairman of the Nuclear Regulatory Commission (NRC), which was in charge of approving nuclear power plant locations and safety checks, about the aging population at the NRC. Meserve answered: "Up to 25 percent of the people are eligible to retire today. We have a situation where we have five times as many people aged over 60 as we have under 30".[10] The decrease in the opportunities of technology transfer, as a consequence of the nuclear power plant accident, greatly restricted the knowledge transfer of the industry.

In Japan, there are three reactor manufacturers: Hitachi Ltd, Toshiba, and Mitsubishi Heavy Industries Ltd. These companies are receiving far fewer orders nowadays, partly because the concern over safety was raised just as in America, and partly because Tokyo Electric Power Company (TEPCO), which foresaw the deregulation of the electric power industry, froze the construction of new power stations. Mitsubishi Heavy Industries Ltd has been suffering especially badly — they have not received any new orders from the Genkai

---

[9]The Three Mile Island Nuclear Generating Station sits on an island in the Susquehanna River in Dauphin County, Pennsylvania, near Harrisburg. It suffered a partial core meltdown.

[10]From "Turning Point of Nuclear Power," *Nikkei Sangyo Shimbun*, July 2001. [Translator's note: It was actually Representative Largent, from the State of Oklahoma, not Representative Tauzin, who asked the question. "Hearing Before the Subcommittee on Energy and Air Quality of the Committee on Energy and Commerce: House of Representatives One Hundred Seventh Congress First Session, 27 June, 2001, Serial No. 107-55," U.S. Government Printing Office, 2001, p. 37.]

Nuclear Power Station (Unit 4) of Kyushu Electric Power Co Inc that was activated in 1997. With the order of Tomari Power Station (Unit 3) of Hokkaido Electric Power Co Inc whose construction work began in 2003, they have barely managed to maintain their technology.

Hitachi Ltd and Mitsubishi Heavy Industries Ltd agreed to cooperate on basic technologies in the nuclear power industry, such as BWR (boiling water reactor) and PWR (pressurized water reactor) on 20 February 2002.[11] Japanese nuclear technology is facing a crisis in securing its knowledge transfer cost.

2.4   Objectives of Knowledge Transfer

Finally, we will consider the motives of knowledge transfer, with the example of an industrial policy.

The Ministry of Economy, Trade and Industry and aircraft manufacturers such as Mitsubishi Heavy Industries Ltd and Kawasaki Heavy Industries Ltd announced their plan of civil aircraft development project.[12] They were aiming to have their airplanes in service by the 2010s, and if they succeeded, it would be the first national passenger airplane for about 40 years since the YS-11.[13] The Japan Defense Agency commenced the domestic development of the next generation models of large transport and antisubmarine aircraft in their New Mid-Term Defense Program in 2001. The estimated total cost of these airplanes was reported to reach 340 billion JPY.

The United States and Europe have traditionally dominated the large aircraft market, and Japanese manufacturers have so far been unable to enter this market. To prevent the demise of Japanese aircraft technology, numerous projects had been planned to develop domestically the next generation mainstay fighters and passenger aircraft, but

---

[11]Hitachi News Releases, "Hitachi and Mitsubishi to Cooperate on Basic Technologies," 20 February 2002.
[12]"National Airplanes to be Developed," *Nihon Keizai Shimbun*, 24 November 2001.
[13]YS-11 was the first airplane that was designed and produced domestically after World War II.

they have never materialized. In fact, the national manufacturers have barely managed to maintain their technology only because the US and European manufacturers shared their technologies with them. These new projects were significant as examples of the government's policy of promoting the preservation of industrial technologies.

As Ryutaro Komiya points out in his book about Japanese industrial policy, "Those industries that the Economic and Industrial Policy Bureau has protected and promoted, judging them profitable to Japan, are in short, connected with the nation's prestige", and these industries are either "symbols of an industrial nation's competency, and are prerequisites of modern nations", or "ones with intrinsic news value".[14]

None of these industries might have been able to grow into what they are now without sufficient protection. The existence of industrial policies demonstrates that more than just a single corporation's profit motive, for example reasons such as, "The industry presents a challenge to the Economic and Industrial Policy Bureau", or "To break through an international monopoly by industrial targeting", affects industrial knowledge transfer.

---

[14] Komiya, Ryutaro, *Industrial Policies in Japan,* Tokyo University Press, 1984.

Chapter 3

Knowledge Transfer Selection

In this chapter, we will examine the conditions for knowledge inheritance and the tendency for the lifespan of knowledge value to shorten in recent years. Also, we will demonstrate that this tendency brings new opportunities for knowledge selection to companies and employees, as well as "new" risks that have not been taken much notice of before.

3.1 Conditions of Knowledge Inheritance

Books recording a particular piece of knowledge are not sufficient proof of knowledge inheritance (see Figure 4), because knowledge does not have any effect on people unless it is understood and made use of. Even if we become able to practice knowledge, there is a limit to our memory (Figure 5), and to our lives too. If we want to preserve a certain piece of knowledge, we have to transfer knowledge from the old to the young.

As we have seen in Chapter 2, there are costs involved in running a knowledge transfer system. A society can bear only so much cost, and learners can spare only so much time. Therefore, not every piece of new knowledge will be inherited. Because of knowledge transfer system costs, the amount of knowledge that can be inherited is necessarily limited.

For example, regional cultures, such as dialects, are gradually disappearing. This may be because communities do not provide the younger generation with the education necessary for the knowledge

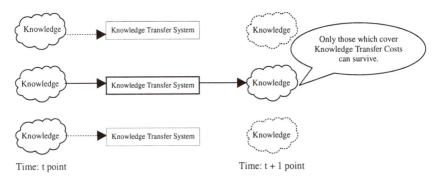

Figure 4:   Knowledge Inheritance Flow Chart

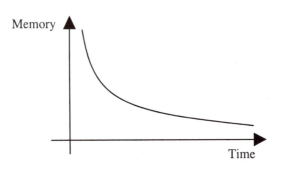

Figure 5:   The Forgetting Curve of Hermann Ebbinghaus

inheritance, or that the youth themselves cannot spare enough time to learn the dialect.

Certain knowledge is passed on to the next generation, while other knowledge disappears without a trace. Publications are an example of a major medium for knowledge inheritance. We will focus on magazine publication here. Table 5 shows the change in number of serial publications (1991–2000).[1] Every year, many new magazines are created, while many existing magazines are lost.

New magazines are published to meet readers' needs, but they disappear if they do not retain the readers' support. Since publishing is a commercial enterprise, if the readers' support, reflected in the

---

[1] Shiozawa, Minobu, *Comparison of Japanese Companies: Publishers*, Jitsumukyoiku-Shuppan, 2001.

Table 5: The Change in the Number of Serial Publications

	1991	1992	1993	1994	1995	1996	1997	1998	1999	2000
Launched Publication	137	140	144	131	177	207	192	170	194	191
Discontinued/Ceased Publication	91	122	152	96	142	100	138	160	148	129

sales, does not cover the maintenance cost, the continuance of that publication becomes endangered.

Similarly, publication of books cannot be sustained if a certain level of sales cannot be expected. If a book is popular and is expected to bring more sales, it will be reprinted. If, on the other hand, the book does not sell well, it is likely to go out of print.

From the analogy of the conditions of book and magazine publications, we can surmise that the essential condition of knowledge inheritance is that the knowledge generates more profit than the costs of its transfer.

This means that in order to pass a certain piece of knowledge down the generations, we need to "reduce the transfer costs", or "create a situation in which the value produced by that knowledge is enhanced".

As we have seen in the previous chapter, sometimes the values of more than just simple commercial activities are reflected in "the value produced by knowledge". For example, unique regional customs might have had values like "securing the integrity of the community", or "building a sense of community". Nowadays, however, they are considered to be a barrier to communications between different regions, and their priority in knowledge inheritance has decreased.

3.2 Occurrence of Knowledge Selection Opportunities

Once the knowledge they possess becomes outdated, employees and companies have to gain new knowledge to make a living. In the computer industry, knowledge becomes obsolete very quickly. The rapid development in workstations has lessened the demands for mainframe computers.[2] This was because it became possible to complete processes, which used to be done by mainframe computers, by workstations that were easier to handle. Recently, high performance personal computers have become widespread, taking over from workstations. Therefore, the knowledge for maintaining and developing programs for mainframe computers has been much less in demand, lessening the career opportunities for those with that particular knowledge.

In the recording media industry, media that have higher capacities and are easier to handle are needed, as the digitization of contents has progressed. Magnetic-storage media such as cassette tapes and floppy disks were once the mainstream portable products, but have now been overtaken by optical storage devices like CDs and DVDs.

In the broadcasting industry in Japan, a shift from analog to digital broadcasts is planned by the end of 2006. Most of the knowledge built up in the era of analog broadcasting will become obsolete, as new broadcasting equipment and receiving apparatus will be introduced.

In fact, there has been a tendency for the lifespan of knowledge (the period of time when knowledge has value) to become increasingly shorter in recent years. Table 6 shows this trend in the lifecycle of knowledge (technology).[3]

According to a survey by the National Institute of Science and Technology Policy, a new technology was valuable for 21.8 years before 1959, but it has been valuable only for 3.2 years since 1990. If the working life of an employee is about 30 years, in the past, he could live on the knowledge of a single technology for most of his career, once he acquired it. Now, he has to learn new technologies every three years.

---

[2]Mainframe computers are usually large-scale computers with functions for business and scientific applications, capable of supporting remote terminals. Workstations are general-purpose microcomputers, often used as a server or host computer on the Internet.
[3]National Institute of Science and Technology Policy, "Assessment of the Effects of R&D Policy on Economic Growth," June 1999, pp. 26, 28 and 30.

Table 6:   Knowledge Lifecycle

	The Period When Knowledge is Profitable (years)	The Time it Takes for Knowledge to be Introduced to the Market (years)	The Period for Research and Development (years)
Before 1959	21.8	1.1	4.5
1960–1969	16.8	1.3	3.8
1970–1979	10.2	1.5	3.9
1980–1989	6.5	1.2	3.4
Since 1990	3.2	0.9	2.6

Generally speaking, high-margin products are those that are in high demand and are solely supplied. If the product is unevenly distributed, it brings profit to the supplier in the process of its percolating through the whole market, and the need for it decreases as it becomes evenly distributed.

By analogy, the background of shortening of knowledge lifespan can be analyzed thus (see Figure 6):

(1) Removal of obstacles to knowledge transfer
(2) Acceleration of knowledge distribution
(3) Shift of product choice from suppliers to consumers

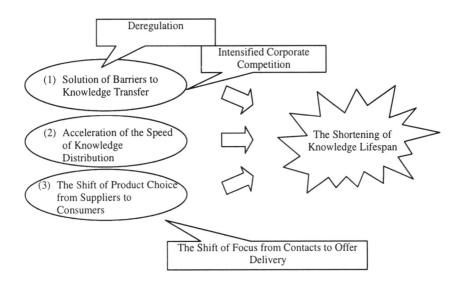

Figure 6:   The Shortening of Knowledge Lifespan

1)   *Removing the obstacles to knowledge transfer*

From the period of reconstruction after World War II and through the
period of high economic growth, the Japanese economy has entered a
new phase of deregulation. As various regulations were eased, which
had previously been adopted to protect and promote national industries and to maintain the quality of products, it became easier for foreign companies to enter the Japanese market, which intensified the
already stiff corporate competition. Firms have to absorb new knowledge before their competitors do, and swiftly dispose of knowledge
that has lost its competitive advantage. With a certain order, valuable
knowledge is copied and becomes evenly distributed, balancing out
differences in corporate competency.

Table 7 is the chronology of deregulation in the "Competition Policy, etc." category.[4] Japan has been promoting competition policies,
with the view of realizing an open and creative international society
by allowing the market mechanism to function. Table 8 shows the
implementation of the "Three-Year Program for Promoting Deregulation (Revised)" by category.[5]

The vested interests in various industries, which have been
hindering knowledge distribution, are being uprooted by the general
relaxation of regulations.

2)   *Acceleration of knowledge distribution*

As the speed of information transmission increases, the time it
takes to recognize a state of unevenly distributed knowledge and to
transmit information to resolve any uneven distribution is shortened.
Improvements in communication tools, such as the development
of telecommunications networks and various other media, have
expanded information distribution dramatically. Table 9 shows the

---

[4]Management and Coordination Agency (Ed.), "White Paper on Deregulation, 2000,"
2000, p. 33.
[5]Management and Coordination Agency (Ed.), "White Paper on Deregulation, 2000,"
2000, p. 8.

Table 7: Chronology of Deregulation in "Competition Policy, etc." Category

Month/Year	Major Deregulation Reforms
June 1990	The Fair Trade Commission (FTC) announced its "Policy on Criminal Accusation Regarding Antimonopoly Violations"
July 1991	An increase in the applicable administrative fines (surcharges) was implemented (from 1.5% to 6%) (3% for small and mid-sized firms) "Review of Exemptions of the Antimonopoly Act" was announced
January 1993	The criminal fines limit was increased (from less than 5 million JPY to less than 100 million JPY)
April 1995	The standard of "Large-scale firms" was raised (from capital of more than 10 billion JPY or net assets of more than 30 billion JPY to capital of more than 35 billion JPY or net assets of more than 140 billion JPY)
April 1996	Review of premium regulations (increase in the upper-limit, etc.)
April 1997	Designation of resale price maintained products (clothes and cosmetics) was cancelled
June 1997	International contract notification procedures were abolished
July 1997	35 Cartel exemptions from the Antimonopoly Acts based on 20 separate acts were abolished or downsized
December 1997	Holding company system was legalized The range of stock that was subject to the large-scale firm stock limit was diminished
January 1999	Merger and share holding notification procedures were revised
July 1999	Antirecession cartels, rationalization cartels, and the exemption systems of the Antimonopoly Act were abolished Antimonopoly Act exemption based on independent acts were further restricted
April 2000	Consumer Contract Law was enacted
May 2000	Revised Antimonopoly Act was enacted, concerning civil remedy to violations (Unfair Trade Practices) of the Antimonopoly Act
June 2000	Article 21 of the Antimonopoly Act (exemption systems for practices unique to natural monopoly) was revoked

Table 8: The Implementation of the Three-Year Program for Promoting Deregulation (Revised) by Category (as of 1 October 1999)

Category	Number of Plans	Number of Plans Executed (A)	Number of Plans Partially Executed (B)	Number of Plans Executed and Partially Executed (A+B)	Number of Plans Not Executed
Competition Policy, etc.	9	3	6	9	0
Housing, Land and Public Works	88	67	17	84	4
Information and Telecommuni-cations	146	80	30	110	36
Distribution	54	24	15	39	15
Transportation	73	42	26	68	5
Standards, Inspection and Import	138	63	40	103	35
Finance, Securities and Insurance	91	54	15	69	22
Energy	36	5	21	26	10
Employment and Labor	38	12	19	31	7
Pollution, Waste and Environmental Preservation	11	6	4	10	1
Explosives and Combustibles, Disaster Prevention and Safety	94	36	41	77	17
Education	52	31	15	46	6
Medical Care and Welfare	45	13	16	29	16
Legal Affairs	18	9	9	18	0
Others	24	9	6	15	9
Total	917(100)	454(49.5)	280(30.5)	734(80.0)	183(20.0)

Table 9:   The Change in Information Turn Volume

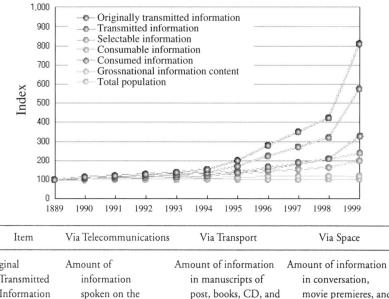

Item	Via Telecommunications	Via Transport	Via Space
Original Transmitted Information	Amount of information spoken on the phone, broadcast on the TV	Amount of information in manuscripts of post, books, CD, and video software	Amount of information in conversation, movie premieres, and drama
Transmitted Information	Amount of information in broadcasting	Total amount of information in publication (books, CD, and video software)	Total amount of information in conversations, movies, and drama at various cinemas and theaters
Selectable Information	Sum of all the information of all broadcasting programs that can be received and selected	Total amount of publication (books, CD, and video software)	Sum of all the information in conversations, movies, and drama performed for each single audience in cinemas and theatres in a year
Consumable Information	Sum of all the information in broadcast programs	Total amount of information in publication (books, CD, and video software)	Sum of all the information in conversations, movies, and drama performed for each single audience in cinemas and theatres in a year

Table 9:   (*Continued*)

Item	Via Telecommunications	Via Transport	Via Space
Consumed Information	Sum of all the information actually consumed in phone conversations, by audience of TV	Sum of all the information people gain from reading books, listening to CD, watching video software	Sum of all the information people have in listening to others in conversations, watching movies and drama

shift in the amount of information in the past 10 years.[6] The amount of originally transmitted information has increased eightfold in 10 years.

An increasing number of people are subscribing to Broadband Internet connections. The Ministry of Internal Affairs and Communications estimated that approximately 24.94 million households would be using Broadband, including FTTH and FWA, by 2005.[7,8] The dissemination of broadband connections improves the speed of information distribution, and further lessens its time cost, as shown in Table 10 and Figure 7.

3)   *Shift of product choice from suppliers to consumers*

When customers purchase products and services, suppliers have more power than customers if resources are limited and a stable supply is needed. In the past, this was the norm in Japan, when resources were imported from abroad and the economy was growing rapidly. Therefore, business connections such as corporate affiliations were important, as they prevented consumers from having a free choice of

---

[6]Ministry of Internal Affairs and Communications (Ed.), "Information and Communications in Japan, White Paper 2001," 2001, pp. 222 and 338.

[7]Ministry of Internal Affairs and Communications (Ed.), "Information and Communications in Japan, White Paper 2001," 2001, p. 14.

[8]FFTH refers to fiber optic service that delivers broadband service to individual homes. FWA stands for Fixed Wireless Access, which uses radio for access to the telephone network and the Internet.

Table 10: Download Time for Contents of Various Types

	ISDN (64 Kbps)	DSL (600 Kbps)	Cable TV (approx. 1.5 Mbps)	FTTH (100 Mbps)
Music (approx. 5 min per song) Approx. 4.8 M (MP3)	approx. 10 min	approx. 64 s	approx. 25.6 s	approx. 0.4 s
Music (approx. 74 min per album) Approx. 72 M (MP3)	approx. 2.5 h	approx. 15 min	approx. 6 min	approx. 6 s
Films (approx. 2 h) Approx. 3.6 G (MPEG2)	approx. 125 h	approx. 13 h	approx. 5 h	approx. 5 min

Source: Ministry of Internal Affairs and Communications (Ed.), "Information and Communications in Japan, White Paper 2001," 2001, p. 10.

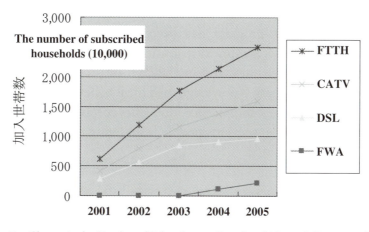

Figure 7: Change in the Number of Subscribers to Broadband Network (Estimation)
Source : Ministry of Internal Affairs and Communications (Ed.), "Information and Communications in Japan, White Paper 2001," 2001, p. 14.

products. With the development of digital and network technologies, however, the value of connections has been reduced. In the film and music industries, which are based on knowledge, the emphasis is shifting from the restrictions of suppliers to needs of consumers. In recent years, this tendency has been most apparent in the IT industry.

Table 11 shows the survey on customer satisfaction in the IT industry.[9] The topmost and second ranked companies are marked. As can be seen, some companies like IBM Japan gain exclusively high degrees of consumer satisfaction.

Figure 8 is the factor analysis of Table 11.[10] We can see that customers have two criteria — "the ability to execute technology (if they execute their business using high technology)" and "ease of communication (if they accommodate unreasonable demands)" — to evaluate vendors. The IT industry's technologies are rapidly changing. Customers may not be able to respond to these changes if they stick to vendors of particular technologies. It is desirable to be able to make amendments even if a decision has already been made. That is why customers value vendors who can execute technologies effectively, and who will cater to their demands even if they are rather unreasonable.

Because of the shortening of knowledge lifespan, people come across multiple knowledge selection opportunities. Especially in recent years, great progress has been made in the elimination of barriers to information distribution, in the acceleration of information transfer rates, and in the shift of product choice from suppliers to consumers. Knowledge shelf life is believed to continue to decrease. Knowledge obsolescence intensifies corporate competition, and at the same time, prevents people from living on the knowledge that they have obtained.

3.3   Examples of Knowledge Selection in Corporations

The electronics industry, which has numerous businesses, including semiconductors and mainframe computers, has taken on an ambitious undertaking.

---

[9] "Sixth Survey on Computer Customer Satisfaction," *Nikkei Computer*, 18 December 2000.

[10] Composed by the authors, based on the survey by *Nikkei Computer*.

Table 11: Customer Satisfaction Survey

Names of Corporations	Development Speed	Meeting the Deadlines	Meeting the Budget	Planning	Job Analysis	Skills	Project Management	Response to Modifications	Quality of Finished Systems	Initial Response to Problems	Trouble Shooting	Fees for Services
IBM Japan	65	67	61	67	66	77	65	59	68	66	66	36
Nihon Unisys	61	70	68	59	65	67	63	63	67	69	65	46
Hitachi	60	63	63	53	56	69	57	59	63	64	62	46
NEC	58	61	62	52	52	64	53	54	59	58	56	45
Fujitsu	57	59	61	54	54	64	55	54	58	56	55	44
Oki Electric Industry	58	70	73	50	61	58	51	67	65	61	67	47
Toshiba	52	63	54	45	43	57	52	43	52	54	52	36
NCR Japan	48	59	61	47	48	54	50	44	58	61	59	35
NTT	61	72	69	62	60	69	61	64	68	69	67	48
NTT Data	58	66	62	61	64	70	59	55	59	60	60	39
NEC Soft	58	60	64	46	49	62	51	58	55	61	56	45
Fujitsu Business Systems Japan	56	53	65	45	49	57	46	53	55	55	50	43
CSK	68	71	65	57	57	65	58	54	61	61	61	42

Source: Ministry of Internal Affairs and Communications (Ed.), "Information and Communications in Japan, White Paper 2001," 2001, p. 278.

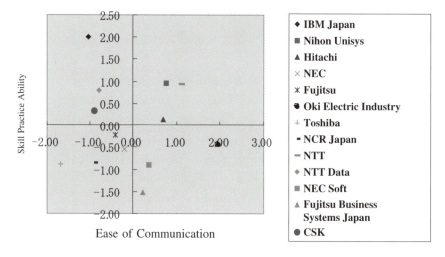

Figure 8:　Positioning Analysis Based on Customer Satisfaction

Electronics manufacturers, such as NEC and Toshiba, have their own semiconductor and mainframe computer projects. However, the mainframe computer industry has stalled, and the semiconductor industry is facing the gravest recession to date. There was a time when semiconductors produced half the profits of an entire company, but with fierce competition from American and Korean companies, the Japanese semiconductor industry is now on its death bed. Therefore, electronics manufacturers are looking to relocate the majority of the staff of mainframe computers and semiconductors to the promising IT sectors, such as servers and system development using PCs.

Fujitsu Group converted an entire floor of a factory into an "IT Training Center" with accommodation facilities, which could house more than 400 people at any one time.[11] It is reported that the manager of the Fujitsu Numazu factory said, "Career change on this scale has never been done before, so a hard-landing is expected to a certain extent". In fact, 30% of the mainly middle-aged and older

---

[11] "Fierce Competition in the IT Service Industry," *Nihon Keizai Shimbun*, 3 November 2001.

employees are expected to be unable to cope with the change.[12] Those who do not manage to adapt to the career change might lose their jobs. One factory worker who has completed the training course said, "The change to systems engineer is like erasing my 15 years of experience at the factory".

Hitachi announced the relegation of its DRAM project to a joint venture with NEC.[13] As for the company's semiconductor project, the focus will be on microcomputers and processors for cellular phones, and they will reduce the workforce by 3100 by the end of 2001.[14] Toshiba announced that they would withdraw from the DRAM business on 18 December 2001.[15] Like Hitachi, Toshiba will specialize in Flash memory and System LSIs, playing on their strengths, and will reduce Memory Department personnel from 4000 to 2000.

In this ever-changing society, there is no guarantee that the estimated profit from the knowledge remains higher than the knowledge transfer costs, even if it is so at present. Knowledge that is vastly profitable at one point may still become obsolete one day.

3.4 Emerging Knowledge Selection Risk

If the lifespan of knowledge is sufficiently long, there will only be few knowledge selection opportunities. Even if that particular knowledge becomes obsolete, you only have to change to knowledge that is valuable at that moment. However, the shortening of knowledge life forces several knowledge selections on people. Furthermore, it

---

[12]"Fujitsu, Remodeling in Major Factories," *Nihon Keizai Shimbun*, 26 December 2001.

[13]DRAM is the acronym for dynamic random access memory. It is the most common kind of random access memory used in personal computers for the main memory. It needs to be refreshed periodically to retain memory.

[14]Hitachi News Releases, "Hitachi to Reconstruct its Semiconductor Business," 10 October 2001.

[15]Toshiba Press Releases, "Toshiba Announces Reorganization of Memory Business," 18 December 2001.

makes knowledge obsolete, and makes it difficult to estimate the value of knowledge in knowledge selection. Because there is a time lag between knowledge selection and the completion of knowledge transfer, no one can say for sure at the stage of knowledge selection which knowledge would create value in the future.

Therefore, knowledge selection entails two risks: the danger that the learner might fail in the knowledge transfer, and the danger that the knowledge might not produce the expected profit. These risks are called "knowledge selection risks" in this book (see Table 12 and Figure 9).

For example, when you decide to learn a new language, it is very difficult to choose which one if you think only in terms of profit. You might find that you do not like the language after you have started studying it, or if competitors increase, you might have to attain a higher level of fluency to gain any profit from the knowledge of the language.

In the IT industry, the great choice is whether you choose Microsoft or Java as the platform for system development. Depending on

Table 12:   Knowledge Selection Risk

Types of Risk	Content
Failure of Transfer	Risk of learner's failing in knowledge transfer
Failure of Profit	Risk of knowledge not producing expected profit

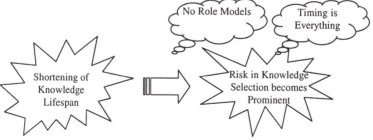

Figure 9:   Emerging Knowledge Selection Risk

future developments in the IT industry, you might win or lose. You might even have to start from scratch again.

3.5 The Acceleration of the Shortening of Knowledge Life by the Evolution of IT Technologies

There have been drastic changes in IT technologies in recent years. The methods of collecting, processing, and analyzing information have completely changed, thus changing the way business is conducted. If not for these changes, we would not have to worry that knowledge which has been acquired would become useless in the near future.

The progress in semiconductor device fabrication, which triggered the IT technology advancements, seems unrelenting. Integration techniques are said to develop at the formidable speed of "18 months doubling" (twice as many transistors can be integrated into a chip in 18 months as before). Some predict that advances in semiconductors will continue until around 2010.[16] As for the ways of using IT technologies, new technologies that facilitate knowledge selection are developed one after another. In this section, we will discuss the developments in the IT industry and their effects on corporate activities.

1) *Developments in the basic technology*

Gordon Moore, one of the founders of Intel, proposed the empirical rule — "the doubling of the number of transistors on integrated circuits every 18 to 24 months" — in 1965. Since then, this rule, Moore's law, has been widely used as the indicator of semiconductor development. This empirical rule and the trends in the network technologies are the key to future IT technology developments.

Semiconductor manufacturers have been announcing various technologies to ensure that Moore's law will still be valid in the future.

---

[16]"The Future of Server System," *Nikkei Computer*, 5 November 2001.

In June 2001, Intel succeeded in completing a prototype transistor of a 20 nm gate length, the linewidth 0.045 μm, using EUV lithography. Intel is planning to shorten the gate length to 16 nm, by using the manufacturing process of linewidth 0.032 μm.

A CMOS Transistor prototype with a gate length of 15 nm by AMD was exhibited at the International Electron Devices Meeting (IDEM) in 2001.[17]

Furthermore, there is research in areas other than microfabrication to enhance semiconductors' processing functions. In June 2001, IBM announced "Development of High-Performance Strained-Silicon-Transistor Technology", which accelerates the current by warping the material of semiconductors. Hitachi announced a similar technique in December 2001.[18] Intel put Simultaneous Multithreading technique to use in 2001, and has adopted this technology in the production of some of their products.

On the other hand, as for networks, an economic rejuvenation policy for optical fiber network was implemented in 1999 (see Figure 10). Speeding up the process planned in the initial plan, the network is constructed so that national coverage is achieved by 2005.

In response to the demand for further increases in speed and volume, basic research for realizing petabit class networks and studies of quantum communication technology were undertaken (see Figures 11 and 12).

2)   *The birth of XML web services*

XML web service technology facilitates communication among independent information processing services on the Internet. The program, which uses the standard protocol of the Internet and can be used from other programs, is called XML web service.

For example, when you make a reservation at a hotel, many hotels allow you to do so easily via the Internet with their own

---

[17] http://pcweb.mycom.co.jp/news/2001/12/07/22.html
[18] Hitachi News Releases, "Development of High-Performance Strained-Silicon-Transistor Technology," 6 December 2001.

Coverage Rate (Target)

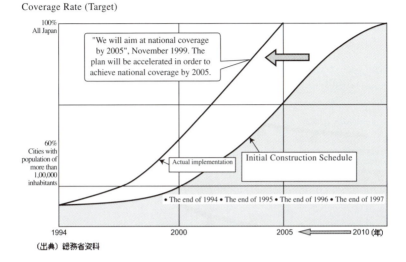

Figure 10: Construction of Optical Fiber Network Infrastructure[19]

A. Research on petabit class photonics transmission and switching technology

Research on transmission technology, utilizing optical fiber's attributes (amplitude, wavelength and phase) to the maximum.
Also, research on switching technology to make petabit class data transmission possible.

B. Research on control technology concerning dynamic network basic technology

Research on traffic control on photonics network regardless of communications protocol will be conducted, to realize control technology that can operate petabit class network effectively.

Figure 11: Summary of the Research on Basic Technology for Petabit Class Network[20]

web applications. However, these web applications require human involvement (see Figure 13).

Instead of a human user, a program may access other programs on the Internet, compare the information, and reserve the best hotel. This is what can be offered by XML web services (see Figure 14).

---

[19] Ministry of Internal Affairs and Communications (Ed.), "Information and Communications in Japan, White Paper 2001," 2001, p. 12.
[20] Ministry of Internal Affairs and Communications (Ed.), "Information and Communications in Japan, White Paper 2001," 2001, p. 277.

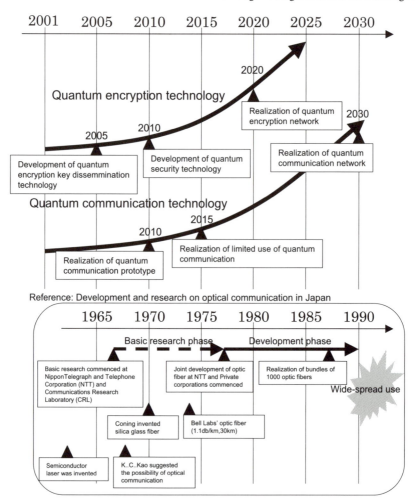

Figure 12: Research and Development Plan for Quantum Communication Technology[21]

In the past, companies were required to have various business systems, such as accounting or sales management systems. However, this entailed a huge cost to construct each system, and besides, business activities have to be reassessed now and again to outperform competing companies. Computer processing power improves daily, quickly obsolescing existing systems.

---

[21] Ministry of Internal Affairs and Communications (Ed.), "Information and Communications in Japan, White Paper 2001," 2001, p. 278.

For example, reserving a room in a hotel, [In the past] Booking by telephone calls or fax. Men checked multiple hotels.

Booking via browsers. Men check multiple URLs.

Automatic booking by programs. Programs check multiple websites.

Figure 13: Things that Web Services Make Possible

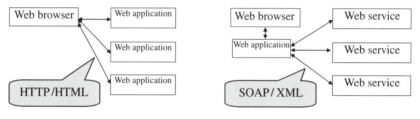

[Web application]
Input and output through Web browsers are required.
Various interfaces.
HTML is difficult to automate because of different data structure and tagged formats.
[Web services]
Programs can communicate with each other without human intervention.
SOAP/XML interface.

Figure 14: Differences between Web Services and Web Applications

With web service technology in general use, however, companies do not have to possess these systems anymore. They only have to secure those information processing services that are at the core of their business, and use other information processing services offered by other companies for the rest. Now it is possible for companies to choose the most appropriate information processing services for

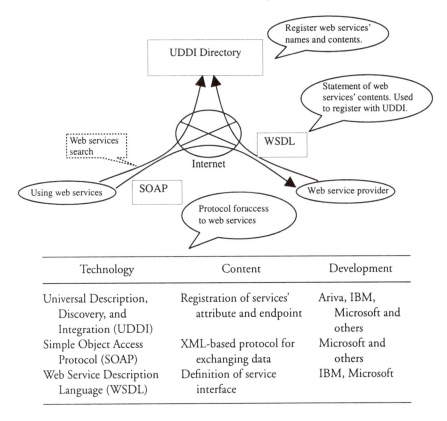

Technology	Content	Development
Universal Description, Discovery, and Integration (UDDI)	Registration of services' attribute and endpoint	Ariva, IBM, Microsoft and others
Simple Object Access Protocol (SOAP)	XML-based protocol for exchanging data	Microsoft and others
Web Service Description Language (WSDL)	Definition of service interface	IBM, Microsoft

Figure 15:   Basic Technology to Realize Web Services

their business, according to the change in the environment. The main infrastructure technologies for web services are shown in Figure 15.

How has corporate management been changed by the realization of web service technologies?

X Corporation engages in sales of stationary via the Internet, for example. In order to run an office that supplies sales business, you need to authenticate customers, settle payments by credit card, promote sales, and manage stock, distribution of goods, personnel, accounting, and customers. In the past, companies used to handle most of the functions noted above themselves, and if they did outsource some of the business to other firms, they had to spend enough time on communication with them to build a solid business relationship. However, these relationships could hinder reassessment of the business and enhancement of the service level.

With web service technology, X Corporation's information processing services can be changed into what is shown in Figure 16. There are companies specializing in information processing services in accounting and personnel management now. Information processing services are becoming just like water or electricity: you only pay for what you use.

X Corporation has only to take care of the core business of their enterprise, and choose the services that best meet their demands for the rest of the business. As a whole, X Corporation can run the business of stationery sales. X Corporation can focus on the core business, and the rest is outsourced to specialists, thus promoting further efficiency.

Most of the standards for web service technologies are world standards. Just as we can view different homepages without worrying about their platforms, we can use web services without worrying about the particular system environment of the programs.

Therefore, if the chosen services are no longer relevant to your company, you only have to choose a relevant one, responding to change in the corporate environment and business strategy. And, you do not need a vast investment for the entire change of systems like before. It can be done with a partial change in the setup.

As the shortening of knowledge shelf life demonstrates, the environment that surrounds corporations is changing rapidly. Those companies that cannot promptly offer products and services that customers want cannot survive in the market.

The CIO of one manufacturer says, "To survive global competition, we have to constantly deal with competitive companies, beyond existing relationships. The ideal is to reassess business relationships every day".[22]

---

[22]"The Dawn of Service-Oriented Era," *Nikkei Computer*, 5 November 2001.

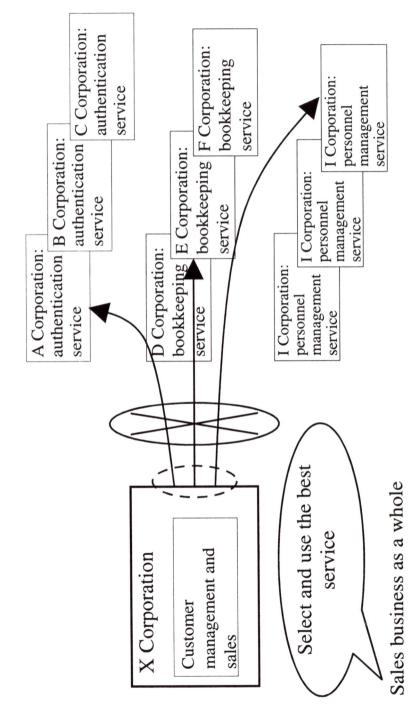

Figure 16:   Application of Information Processing Services

XML web service technology offers system infrastructure for companies to compete against the shortening of knowledge profitability and to prompt selection of services, thus further escalating the obsolescence of knowledge that forms the foundation of services.

Chapter 4

The Impact of Knowledge Selection

In this chapter, we will argue that with the shortening of knowledge lifespan and the increasing difficulty in the prediction of knowledge profitability, it is becoming harder for organizations to advocate secure employment for all employees as their management policy. Under these circumstances, employees will be forced to make multiple choices of knowledge selection to enhance their expertise.

4.1   The Effect of Knowledge Selection on Organizations

Since knowledge is "that which is lost unless deliberately maintained", it is cultivated and used for business by members of organizations. If there is no merit in belonging to an organization, there is no point in forming one for members who possess knowledge.

Table 13 shows the merits that members of organizations (called "employees" hereafter) usually expect from "organizations".

On the other hand, as the conditions for offering those merits to their employees, "organizations" expect employees to possess either the knowledge necessary for their business or the ability to acquire it. Therefore, conditions for employees to belong to organizations can be illustrated as in Table 14.

Having employees who satisfy those conditions facilitates the development of corporate enterprises, and belonging to organizations which provide these requirements gives security to employees' lives.

Organizations consist of more than just employees. For example, the stakeholders of an organization such as stockholders, suppliers

47

Table 13:   Expectations of Employees from Organizations

Types of Merits	Content
Providing livelihood	Organizations provide employees with financial security, based on knowledge that employees possess
Providing opportunities of knowledge transfer	Organizations provide employees with opportunities for acquiring know knowledge (time, money, and knowledge transfer systems)
Providing opportunities of knowledge usage	Organizations provide employees with opportunities for using knowledge

Table 14:   Expectations of Organizations from Employees

Types of Merits	Content
Practice of knowledge	Employees provide organizations with knowledge necessary for business

and customers can be named as factors concerning the organization. From the viewpoint of the organizational equilibrium theory, organizations are understood to exist only when they are able to maintain relationships among these factors and remain profitable ("merits from participating in the organization" minus "contribution to the organization"). This sounds reasonable enough. Each factor continues to have a relationship with the organization because it gives them some benefits. Hence, it can be deduced that the "continuance of organizations through knowledge selection" is equal to "maintenance of the (merits − contribution > 0) inequality in the process of new knowledge selection".

Figure 17 is a simplified chart of balance in organizations. In which factor of the organization the maximum pressure is piled on in knowledge selection depends on who has taken the initiative in the decision making.

For example, if the owner (stockholder) of an organization had taken the initiative, he would prompt the organization to adjust its business so that he could secure a return on investment at a certain

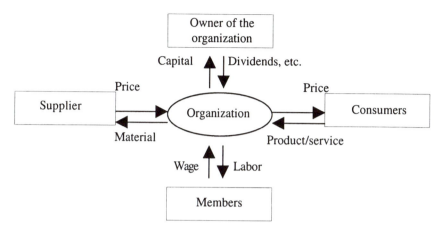

Figure 17:   Diagram of Organizational Equilibrium

rate. When there is a change in the business, its products will be changed, and the knowledge required will be different. These would be sourced inside and outside the organization. If the employees could not gain new knowledge, they would have to be replaced. The organization would need a new supplier for new products, too. The new market would bring new customers.

On the other hand, if employees showed the initiative, they would focus on the security of their jobs and the duties required of them. It would be highly unlikely that organizations would acquire new knowledge at a speed beyond the employees' ability to learn it. Since the owners bear the cost of training, their share of profit would be reduced. Owners of organizations that are not producing enough profit might sell their stock.

If suppliers or customers showed the initiative, they would refuse choices that supplanted existing products, by preferring their own products or ones that suited their tastes.

Wherever the pressure is, depending on who has taken the initiative in the organization, knowledge selection disturbs the equilibrium within the organization. It also has the impact of undermining the existing business model. Knowledge selection disrupts the continuity of organizations.

4.2   The Conditions of the Lifetime Employment System

In this section, we will discuss the influence that the decrease in knowledge lifespan has on the lifetime employment system.

The prerequisites for maintaining the lifetime employment system are that: (a) knowledge transfer costs for the existing employees can be covered, and (b) knowledge selection risks can be accepted, when organizations face knowledge selection opportunities. Unless these two conditions are met, the lifetime employment system cannot be sustained.

1)   *Organizations with single knowledge*

We will simulate this with a simple example. We define the objective of Organization A as its continual existence, and it possesses a single piece of knowledge. If the cost of organizational maintenance can be covered by the profit from the knowledge, the organization is able to survive.

The costs for (i) knowledge transfer is (Ai), and the cost for maintaining the organization (personnel cost, etc.) is (Bi). The profit produced by knowledge that is gained from (i) knowledge transfer is (Ci), and the rate of gaining that profit is (Pi). This organization plans knowledge transfer when its knowledge becomes obsolete, and the cost for gaining new knowledge is born by the profit from the knowledge that has previously been profitable.

For Organization A to survive, profit (Ci) has to surpass the total value of maintenance cost (Bi) and the next knowledge transfer cost (Ai + 1).

If the difference is distributed as dividends outside the organization, security of employment will be endangered once this inequality becomes unsustainable. Since profit from knowledge is not stable, if in each knowledge selection the profit of the chosen knowledge becomes 0 at the rate of $(1 - P_1)$, $(1 - P_2)$ and so on, the inequality becomes untrue at the rate of $\{1 - P_1 \times P_2 \times \cdots\}$. The more knowledge selection opportunities there are, the less chance the organization has to survive.

For organizations with single knowledge to maintain the lifetime employment system and continue their existence, they have to retain the profits (income — costs of the next knowledge transfer) or be able to borrow funds when they are running low on capital.

Even if they have great insight into selecting knowledge of great value, a smooth knowledge transfer is not guaranteed, as not every employee is suited for the new knowledge. Employees might rebel against the knowledge transfer, or the massive costs involved in knowledge transfer might grievously restrict the choices of new knowledge.

It is very difficult for organizations with single knowledge to survive in this climate, when knowledge is becoming increasingly less durable, unless they are fortunate enough to generate substantial profits and the owners are considerate enough, for example, to forgo their dividends.

Running organizations with single knowledge is like making a living by hunting. Life is good as long as there is plenty of prey, but once there is a change in the environment, such as the coming of the Ice Age, they have to reconsider their way of life.

2) *Organizations with multiple knowledge (diversification)*

There is a tactic to maintain stable employment by possessing multiple pieces of knowledge. Even if some of the knowledge an organization possesses is not producing a profit, as long as profits from other pieces of knowledge keep the total balance in the black, they can maintain secure employment and continue their existence.

There are, however, four obstacles to this scheme under the current situation of shortening knowledge lifespan.

a) *Negative effect of existing knowledge*

Existing knowledge sometimes hinders the absorption of new knowledge. If the new knowledge becomes dominant, the infrastructure and systems for the old knowledge become unnecessary. Also, since knowledge needs people to practice it, knowledge selection necessarily involves personnel issues. When electric locomotives were introduced in England, train companies could not fire stokers for steam locomotives. So stokers existed long after steam locomotives were gone.

As a piece of knowledge becomes more profitable, it gains influence on the organization — the infrastructure and systems inside the organizations are optimized for the knowledge, and the outlook of the organization becomes influenced by it. Therefore, when new knowledge that surpasses the old knowledge appears, organizations tend to hold on to the old knowledge as they are not able to recognize the new knowledge's value.

This tendency also explains the idea of "the advantage of those that do not possess". England, which developed first as an industrial country, was consequently overtaken by America and Japan. Latecomers to economic competitions commonly lack the infrastructures, practices and systems of the advanced countries. But there are quite often vested interests produced by these older systems and infrastructures, working against attempts at drastic changes to these existing systems. Systems that have functioned well are difficult to discard, which only leads to higher write-off costs in the end.

Of course, if the knowledge's lifespan is sufficiently enduring, or if there is continuity between the old and the new knowledge, the existing infrastructure and systems may well become competitive assets. However, when knowledge becomes short-lived and disruptive, existing systems become obstacles to innovation and change.

Conversely, if the new knowledge is not held back by existing systems, it has the advantage of not having to shoulder the write-off costs of obsolete systems.

b)   *Limited resources*

If an organization could divide resources among all knowledge, it would grow in line with the national economy. However, it is impossible to develop all knowledge, and the resources one organization has are limited, too.

In 2001, the consolidated net sales of Hitachi surpassed eight trillion JPY, and the number of its subsidiaries and affiliated companies amounted to approximately 1100[1]; these included trading, distribution and credit card companies, and even a monorail manufacturer.[2] Hitachi claimed to account for more than 1% of national GDP. Despite its subsidiaries covering a wide range of fields and possessing the most researchers of any Japanese company, Hitachi did not manage to gain the initiative in the recently and rapidly developing areas of OS and CPU for PCs, or video game machines.

In the past, most leading companies in Japan adopted the full line-up strategy. This, however, often led to excessive competition, and it allowed small companies specializing in areas that leading corporations were not strong in to grow into competent rivals, since it was impossible to have every single factor in the production line up-to-date.

Knowledge investment covers too extensive an area, and the resources of companies are too limited. This leads to an uneven distribution of investment in knowledge, causing knowledge to produce insufficient profit.

Since the long recession of the 1990s, most Japanese companies have come to face corporate rationalization and reorganization under slogans such as "Selection and Concentration".

c) *Diversity of competitors*

Competitors over a certain product may not share the same values. One organization may adopt the lifetime employment system, while another may have a very different employment policy.

---

[1] 1069 subsidiaries, 83 affiliated companies. From Hitachi Ltd, "Financial Statement Report, Fiscal Year Ended 31 March 2001," 2001.
[2] Hitachi announced that a part of its shares of Tokyo Monorail would be sold to JR East Japan on 20 December 2001.

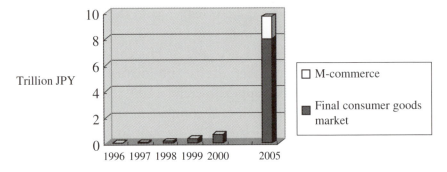

Figure 18:   Size of E-Commerce Market (Final Consumer Goods)[3]

Recent progress in the digital and network industries promoted the e-commerce market, increasing corporate competition in all services (not just industrial products) to the global scale.

As we can see in Figure 18, the e-commerce market is expected to continue its rapid growth, causing increasingly fierce competition among companies all over the world.

Organizations with lifetime employment systems are at a disadvantage in this era in terms of the speed in entering a new market and the quality of the newly gained knowledge, when knowledge's profitability is increasingly less durable, and when consumers value the usefulness of new knowledge more than stable business relations.

d) *Investors' initiative*

When interests are lessened to safeguard unprofitable knowledge, there is a potential harm to the credibility of the firm, lowering the investment in the company. Japanese companies traditionally followed a cross-shareholding system; investment efficiency was not a vital matter. However, the issues of bad debt and the limits on banks' shareholdings have pressured companies to abolish the cross-shareholding system (see Table 15).

---

[3]Ministry of Internal Affairs and Communications (Ed.), "Information and Communications in Japan, White Paper 2001," 2001, p. 51.

Table 15:   Sales of Cross-Shareholdings by Major Banks (March 2002, billion JPY)[4]

	Operation Plan	Business Performance of the First Half of the Year
UFJ	13,825	7,825
B. Mizuho	13,500	4,500
Mitsubishi Tokyo	8,236	2,436
Asahi	4,690	1,690
Mitsui Sumitomo	3,200	1,600
Chuo Mitsui Shintaku	4,856	856
Sumitomo Shintaku	1,742	742
Daiwa	1,489	389
Total	51,500	20,038

ROE has been in use as an indicator of corporate management as economies have become globalized.[5] In Japan, the Defined Contribution Pension Law was enacted in 2001. This system enabled employees to select their pension plans and plan how to manage them, although they will have to bear investment risk. Japanese society has been remodeled with a focus on investment efficiency, down to the grass-root level. If management adopts a policy, unduly valuing employees at the cost of dividends, investors may well lose faith in the organization.

Therefore, sustaining both knowledge transfer costs and a lifetime employment system is hardly viable when not much profit is expected from knowledge and it becomes obsolete quickly. In other words, lifetime employment is only suited for a very unique environment in which the national economy is growing steadily, knowledge life is long, and there are preceding models in knowledge transfer, as there was for Japan after World War II.

---

[4] "Cross-Holding Shares of More than Five Trillion Yen Sold," *Nikkei Kinyu Shimbun*, 6 December 2001.
[5] ROE stands for "Return on Equity": an indicator of profitability. It is calculated by dividing net income over the past 12 months by average stockholders' equity.

4.3   New Behavior Pattern

Lifetime employment and seniority-based pay systems have been characteristics of the employee–company relationship in Japan. From the perspective of stable employment, these systems are very effective. However, the premises for these systems are no longer valid.

After World War II, Japan had successful predecessors in other countries to look to, and had only to follow their examples in knowledge transfer. The government adopted industrial protection policies, allowing companies to focus on expanding their business and acquiring new technologies. Furthermore, the national economy followed a steady upward path, with a constant and high demand for human resources. Knowledge was durable for longer periods than it is now, which enabled employees to build on one particular piece of knowledge as they gained more experience. The seniority-based payment system was valid under these premises.

The shortening of knowledge's durability overthrows these premises. It is no longer possible to build up one's career in a single company for life. Companies have to inject human resources who possess appropriate knowledge promptly so as not to miss business opportunities, and they can no longer be self-contained in terms of personnel training.

What action strategy should employees adopt when organizations abandon the lifetime employment system? Employees are facing the following conditions:

(1) Their existing knowledge will one day be obsolete.
(2) There is no guarantee that they can acquire knowledge that will prove profitable without fail within the present organization.
(3) If the present organization takes a dive in profitability, they will lose their positions.

When employees under these conditions lose their jobs, there are only two options for them — either get another job in a different company on the strength of the existing knowledge, or gain new knowledge. However, it might prove difficult to find another position when the knowledge they possess is already outdated, and the costs of new knowledge transfer are too high without the support of an organization.

Therefore, employees should try to expand the variety of knowledge they possess before they find themselves in this dilemma. Say there are three choices of knowledge, each with an 80% chance of profitability. Roughly speaking, a person with knowledge A only has 80% of profitability, but the rate can be maximized to 99.2% if he has all three pieces — knowledge A, B and C.

The issue arising here is whether it is possible to acquire other knowledge while in the current organization, or after leaving the organization. According to the 2001 "Survey on Companies Utilizing IT and on the Labor Conditions in Information-Related Companies" by the Japan Institute of Labor, 22.2% of companies answered that IT training was "very necessary", and 63.3% answered "necessary". However, they also answered that obstacles to IT training were "Not sufficient time for training" (mid-level management 47.5%, general office employees 37.7%), and "Too costly" (mid-level management 24.1%, general office employees 24.7%), thus showing that there are still insufficient opportunities to gain knowledge in the IT industry.

Workers have to fortify themselves against knowledge obsolescence with multiple knowledge in this era when knowledge lifespan is shortening. If there are organizations which restrict their employees' opportunities to gain new knowledge because they cannot afford to as they are struggling against falling profits, these organizations should reconsider their own *raison d'etre*. If they accept low return orders for the sake of securing employment, this only helps to deprive personnel of development opportunities.

Who should decide what new knowledge to acquire, if employees are to possess multiple knowledge? Information is everywhere, and companies' advantage in information over individuals is lessening. It is becoming harder even for companies to judge which knowledge will yield profits in the future. Besides, companies can no longer guarantee secure employment to their employees, as we have seen in the previous section. If they force their own judgment in knowledge selection on their employees, they cannot afford the possible consequences. Employees have diverse characters, with different kinds of knowledge suitable for different employees. They should select knowledge at their own risk. This means that each individual employee has to face knowledge selection risks.

The issues here are how much knowledge selection risk employees can accept and how they can contain it within that limit. Companies cannot bear all the risks anymore. After selecting the knowledge to acquire, employees have to assess the pertinent risks and prepare hedges against them.

For that purpose, employees have to carefully analyze which knowledge (experience) is their breadwinner. That is, they have to consider: (1) how much longer that knowledge will be valuable; (2) what further knowledge is necessary to obtain their ideal social positions; (3) how much knowledge transfer cost and knowledge selection risk are involved in acquiring that knowledge; and (4) how much risk can be controlled.

It is no longer possible to rely on one job for life. We have to reconsider our approaches towards self-development and organizations. Given that the infrastructures and techniques to manage knowledge selection risks are not yet developed, the situation appears even bleaker.

Part 2

HOW TO MANAGE KNOWLEDGE SELECTION RISK

In Part 2, we will point out tasks that we face as knowledge selection risks emerge, and we will introduce infrastructures that society should be provided with to manage knowledge selection risks, as well as techniques for companies to reduce knowledge selection risks.

Chapter 1

Tasks of Knowledge Selection Society

As we have seen in Part 1, most companies nowadays have to abandon the lifetime employment policy, and employees have to seek opportunities to gain new knowledge independently from their organizations, as the lifespan of knowledge decreases and the profitability of knowledge becomes insecure. This has the potential of overthrowing the national structure of education and employment.

Knowledge selection risks consist of the danger of failing in knowledge transfer, and the danger of the knowledge not returning the expected profit.

For the former risk, there are those tasks such as securing the necessary time, paying the fiscal costs and enhancing the efficiency of knowledge transfer, to alleviate the risk. For the latter, the tasks are: expand demand, predict demand accurately, and so on (see Table 16).

Table 16:   Tasks for Reducing Knowledge Selection Risks

Types of Risk	Tasks for Reducing the Risk
Alleviating knowledge transfer failure risk	- Secure time cost - Secure fiscal cost - Improve knowledge transfer efficiency (study efficiency)
Alleviating low return risk	- Visualize knowledge - Enhance demands - Match demands and supplies - Predict demands accurately - Create knowledge

Social agreement will be necessary to determine how much knowledge transfer cost should be incurred, and by whom and how. Companies cannot bear too much, and individual employees cannot shoulder everything. But if nothing is done, unprofitable knowledge assets in organizations will be steadily accumulated. This would lead to a demise of even a leading company in time.

In Part 2, we will suggest measures to control knowledge selection risks that society should be provided with, and the framework of the new society, through the following four themes:

• **Visualization of knowledge (construction of supply chain management for knowledge)**

In order to be justly evaluated according to its purpose, knowledge and its related information need to be disseminated among people. We will discuss the tasks necessary for the visualization of knowledge and give some examples.

• **Knowledge demand–supply matching (introduction of personnel supply derivatives)**

The estimation of knowledge's value is sometimes affected by the motives of individuals. This causes an imbalance between the demand and supply of knowledge. We will introduce the idea of personnel supply derivative business as a measure to correct this imbalance.

• **Securing knowledge transfer costs (work-sharing, knowledge transfer time)**

A knowledge transfer necessitates the knowledge transfer costs. How to allocate them (particularly the associated time costs) among society, firms and each individual would be one of the important themes in constructing a new, sustainable society. In addition, a work-sharing endeavor which helps alleviate the elevation of unemployment will be explored as a means of allocating the knowledge transfer costs.

- **Efficacy of knowledge transfer systems**

Efficient knowledge transfer with less time and cost is vital in this climate of shortening knowledge lifecycle. Needless to say, the learner has to have an avid interest in the new knowledge, but there are other important techniques to acquire new knowledge in a limited time frame. We will discuss the importance of knowledge transfer system efficiency and give some examples.

Visualization of Knowledge Demand

2.1   The Current Situation

It is difficult to analyze if there is demand for a particular piece of knowledge as we do not know which organization needs what kind of knowledge, or where we can source the people with the necessary knowledge. Quite often in job listings, exactly what kind of personnel are needed is left unclear, except in software and other industries where specific qualifications are a prerequisite. This leads to job listings being incorrectly targeted and companies interviewing the wrong candidates. Sometimes, because of this uncertainty in requirements, those who are planning a new knowledge transfer may be unable to grasp which knowledge is obsolete and which is not, and applicants may join the wrong companies.

2.2   Solutions (Supply Chain Management for Knowledge)

In this section, we will propose a system for sharing information on supply/demand data among interested parties, and discuss the importance of advisory institutions that offer interpretation of information to corporate and individual clients.

1)   *Standardization of knowledge*

Individual users need to have some idea of what the knowledge is about if they are to obtain new knowledge. For that purpose, knowledge has to be defined and designated. Also, for the acquired knowledge to be used in different organizations, terms and criteria have to be standardized. When knowledge is standardized, its usage will increase and its demand will expand.

In scholarship, knowledge is standardized by the systematic compilation of textbooks. In business, it is conducted by "standardization", sorting the knowledge necessary to each business.

For example, the Ministry of Economy, Trade and Industry in Japan made "IT skill standards" public, as the index for the IT skills necessary for IT related services. This was an attempt to establish a framework for the training of IT specialists, itemizing the skills necessary to offer IT services and sorting them objectively and practically.

IT services are divided into several "types of jobs", each with its "performance index" and "skills". "Skills" are further itemized into "proficiency level" and "knowledge". There is also a "skill framework" offering an overall picture of the IT skill index.

Electronic manufacturers, including Hitachi, Toshiba, Matsushita and NEC, have set up a job training scheme for their union members.[1] The objective of this scheme is to facilitate mid-career job change both within one company and within the industry. Union members can avail themselves of language courses and other courses designed to help them gain specific qualifications, held by those companies. By introducing qualifications, the skills of union members who have completed the courses can be seen, facilitating career change within the industry.

2) *Visualization of personnel information*

To enable successful knowledge selection, it is vital to assess the performance of the person who practices the knowledge, as well as the knowledge itself. Most Japanese companies used to withhold information about their employees' abilities. This might have worked

---

[1] "Hitachi, Toshiba, and other Electronics Manufacturers Set Up Training Courses," *Nihon Keizai Shimbun*, 2 January 2002.

well in the lifetime employment system, where employees competed against each other, playing by their own companies' rules. However, it is not very rational if employees are to choose knowledge that will be their own personal asset.

NEC has made the duties and responsibilities of management level employees (approximately 12,000 employees) internally public online.[2] Since salary is determined by duties, all employees can now grasp how much management is paid.

Fuji Xerox has an intriguing scheme.[3] It was reported that they would start a new scheme, in which employees' market value would be calculated by an external institution and reported back to the employees. They would also publish duties, responsibilities and standards for payment, just like NEC.

3) *Supply chain management for knowledge*

A proactive standards agency in the industry would help in the standardization of knowledge, as it is beyond a single individual company's power to establish industry standards, which requires an intimate knowledge of the needs of interested parties. A system will be needed to share information among people who use a particular piece of knowledge and to augment its standardization. This is called Supply Chain Management for Knowledge (SCMK).

In the manufacturing industry, groups of parties involved in the production and distribution of products are called "supply chains". Supply chains manage supply/demand information and inventory, so that they can maximize sales and minimize inventory. This is called Supply Chain Management (SCM), a scheme which builds networks within the chain and manages the data concerning production, inventory, and sales and planning at each level, so that inventory at all levels can be optimized.

---

[2] "NEC Internally Published Management Grade Responsibilities," *Nihon Keizai Shimbun*, 28 March 2002.
[3] "Fuji Xerox: Assessment of Employee Marketability," *Nikkei Sangyo Shimbun*, 1 April 2002.

This works well for manufacturing. However, it might not when it comes to human resources. Knowledge is practiced by human beings. Men cannot be stored in storehouses like product parts. Companies have to be provided with the right number of personnel at the exact moment.

It would improve the visibility of knowledge demand if knowledge demand in companies is analyzed, and if that data are shared among the knowledge supply chains, which consist of recruitment companies, educational institutes and interested employees (see Figure 19).

Many companies are currently working on the construction of SCM concerning parts and material supply. They only have to include knowledge in their SCM schemes. By using this new scheme, SCMK, companies will be able to convey their knowledge demand to their supply chains. By sharing supply and demand information, all parties involved can optimize their supply/demand planning.

Furthermore, if recruitment companies are involved in other companies' SCMK, they would also be able to promote the standardization of knowledge using the data on other companies' needs and convey generalized needs to educational institutions.

In the past, when companies hired new graduates as engineers, some companies allocated the numbers of positions to each school and demanded school recommendations. This can be thought as a type of personnel supply chain between companies and schools. This practice, however, left the standard for personnel assessment and demand information unclear, making it almost impossible to attempt standardization of information on the supply side. The only options applicants had were "companies", not positions. If knowledge supply chains could be constructed, the supply and demand of knowledge would be visualized, strongly propelling knowledge standardization.

There are examples of cooperation between "educational institutions and recruitment agencies" and between "educational institutions and companies", such as AMS Japan and Temp Staff,[4]

---

[4]"AMS Japan and Temp Staff Collaborate in IT Personnel Training," *Nihon Keizai Shimbun*, 6 January 2002.

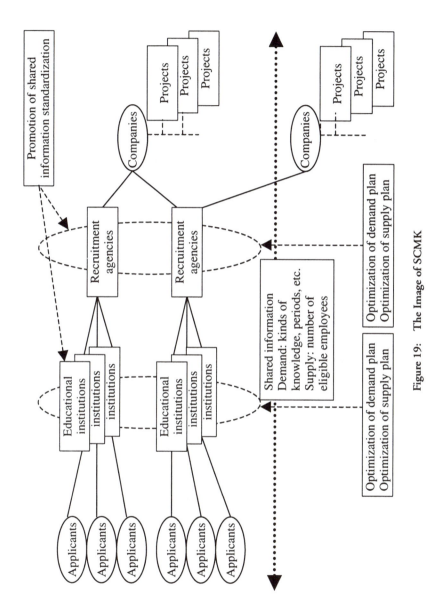

Figure 19: The Image of SCMK

Digital Hollywood's consortium,[5] and Manpower Japan's online staffing business.[6]

AMS Japan, a personnel training company, collaborates with Temp Staff, a recruitment agency, in the area of IT personnel. AMS Japan offers special courses to personnel registered with Temp Staff, and Temp Staff sends members who have gained specialist knowledge through these courses to client companies. In one of the training courses, "Net Professional (campaign basic)", they teach applicants how to construct networks, for example, how to connect cables, and techniques required for CCNA, one of the qualifications granted by Cisco Systems.

Digital Hollywood, an IT engineer training school, has formed a consortium called "Digital Hollywood Partners" with 20 major corporations, such as Matsushita Electric Industrial Co Ltd. Digital Hollywood recommends its students and graduates as on-the-job trainees or permanent employee candidates to the companies, and the companies develop courses such as CRM and Marketing together, when there is demand for them, and market them for in-house training too. The consortium facilitates procurement of personnel with a basic knowledge of IT technology. Personnel, therefore, will not need training after joining the companies. The consortium also holds gatherings that offer opportunities for member companies to exchange information.

Manpower Japan developed a system to manage a variety of information through the Internet, from information about business with client companies to data on staff's working hours. This is called "Manpower E-solutions", and it enables companies to type in duty and types of job, qualifications, positions and fees, to receive information from Manpower concerning the status of the recruitment process.

---

[5] "Collaboration of Major IT Engineer Training Firms," *Nihon Keizai Shimbun*, 21 January 2002.
[6] "Online Temporary Staffing Business, Manpower," *Nikkei Sangyo Shimbun*, 28 January 2002.

As for knowledge standardization for the purpose of sharing information, three major companies, including Pasona, Temp Staff and Recruit Staffing, decided to standardize their online application systems, enabling clients to use the same format for types of job, proficiency, methods of charging fees, and management of actual working hours of temping staff.[7]

4) *Personnel suppliers and career planning advisors*

As various information about the supply and demand of knowledge or about knowledge transfer is shared among concerned parties, it becomes important to interpret the gained information accurately. Specialist advice would be a great help to generate profits, further enhancing the visibility of knowledge. As employees and companies are not familiar with information about knowledge, they can select knowledge more efficiently in choosing new personnel or in designing their career paths, if they are provided with specialist advice. The demand for advisors is expected to increase in the future.

There is no example of advisors specializing in supply–demand information analysis as of yet, but in terms of out-placement counseling, there is the case of Japan Drake Beam Morin (DBM Japan).[8] DBM Japan started a training course for career counselors in April 2002. In this course, students learn basic information about employment, mental health care for job applicants, and know-how for out-placement during the three months of the course, and are then granted a qualification from DBM Japan.

---

[7] "Online Application to be Standardized in June," *Nihon Keizai Shimbun*, 12 April 2002.
[8] "DBM Japan to Join the Career Counselor Business," *Nihon Keizai Shimbun*, 3 January 2002.

Chapter 3

Matching of Knowledge Supply and Demand

3.1   The Current Situation

A company will suffer from a dilemma if it meets a practitioner of knowledge who is needed for a project that has not yet commenced. If they wait until the project is officially launched, other companies might hire the personnel, but if they hire him before the official inauguration of the project, there is a risk that the project may never materialize.

Also, if the prospect of knowledge bearing profit is lowered, learners may hesitate to choose that knowledge, resulting in difficulties in personnel procurement for companies when there is demand for that particular knowledge. Is there any way of facilitating the distribution of knowledge (personnel), whilst lowering the low-return risk of knowledge?

3.2   Solutions (Personnel Supply Derivative Business)

In this section, we will propose employment transactions modeled on financial derivatives, and explain how to manage the knowledge selection risks when this model is used.

1)   *Introduction of personnel supply derivative business*

When knowledge is standardized and a market is formed where supply/demand information can be matched, it is possible to reserve personnel who possess knowledge, or to draw "supply option"

Table 17:   Personnel Supply Derivative Business

Personnel Contract	Content
Personnel supply option	Contract concerning rights to supply, or to be supplied, personnel with particular knowledge for a certain period of time
Personnel supply reservation	A right to supply personnel with particular knowledge for a certain period of time
Personnel supply swap	Contract to mutually exchange personnel with certain knowledge

contracts, based on the standardized knowledge. Table 17 shows an example of a personnel supply derivative contract.

If personnel supply options are available, it becomes possible to guarantee personnel supply at low cost by setting up appropriate conditions of use. Also, through personnel supply reservation, personnel can be stably supplied and positions can be secured, regardless of supply and demand in the market. Personnel supply swap enables the correction of uneven personnel distribution among companies.

As for temporary employment, the Labor Standards Law (amended) (enacted in 1998, implemented in April 1999) allowed employees in highly specialized areas to negotiate contracts of up to three years; this included doctors, scholars, lawyers and chartered accountants. Subsequently, in December 2001, the Council for Regulatory Reform published "Remarks on Regulatory Reforms", arguing that areas of specialist jobs should be further expanded.[1]

In real life, there have been examples of outsourcing personnel for intellectual labor, using contract temping staff.[2] Kao Corporation was reported to have drawn up nondisclosure agreements with about a dozen of temping staff holding master's degrees or doctoral degrees for highly specialized jobs in the composition and analysis of chemical products in spring 2001.

---

[1] "Temporary Staffing: Professional Career to be Expanded," *Nihon Keizai Shimbun*, 28 January 2002.
[2] "Employment Fault 2," *Nihon Keizai Shimbun*, 24 December 2001.

Canon also outsources 7100 employees, out of which 1700 personnel are engaged in research and development departments. Personnel supply derivative contracts provide various solutions to corporations needing different personnel at different times (see Figure 20).

Fullcast, a recruitment agency, has announced that they would enlarge the number of registered staff for catering establishments to approximately 10,000 members by 2004.[3] As staff turnover is high and the business fluctuates seasonally in the catering industry, Fullcast would prepare an expeditious supply of personnel, providing registered staff with training before sending them to client establishments.

As for other similar personnel supply option systems, there is the example of the Self-Defense Forces reserve. The reserve system was established in 1954 to secure personnel for Self-Defense Forces by engaging reserve forces as SDF personnel. A monthly wage of 4000 JPY and a daily training fee of 8100 JPY are paid to Reserve forces.[4]

2)   *Measures for career planning*

The personnel supply derivative business is expected to contribute to the stabilization of the labor market, and to produce new business ideas for personnel management. Conventionally, the career paths of employees were passively formed under the lifetime employment system. The personnel supply derivative business would enable employees to actively plan their career paths (see Figure 21).

For example, each individual receives option fees for a certain period of time in his future through personnel supply reservation contracts or supply option contracts with companies through recruitment agencies, alleviating the low-return risk of knowledge to a certain extent. It provides companies with personnel with the

---

[3]"Powerful Ally of Busy Drinking and Eating Establishments, Fullcast: Registered Members 10,000," *Nihon Keizai Shimbun*, 1 April 2002.
[4]http://www.jda.go.jp/j/defense/yobiji/yobiji.htm

(1) Personnel supply option (in the case of calls)

Corporations pay option fees to purchase rights to hire practitioners of knowledge X for a certain period of time from a certain date. Recruitment agencies have the responsibility of supplying them with personnel as promised when they exercise their rights.

(2) Personnel supply reservation

Corporations pay reservation fees to reserve practitioners of knowledge X for employment for a certain period of time from a certain date. Recruitment agencies have the responsibility of supplying them with personnel as promised.

(3) Personnel supply reservation

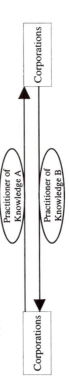

Corporations exchange practitioners of knowledge A with practitioners of knowledge B for a certain period of time.

Figure 20:   Personnel Supply Derivative Contract Model

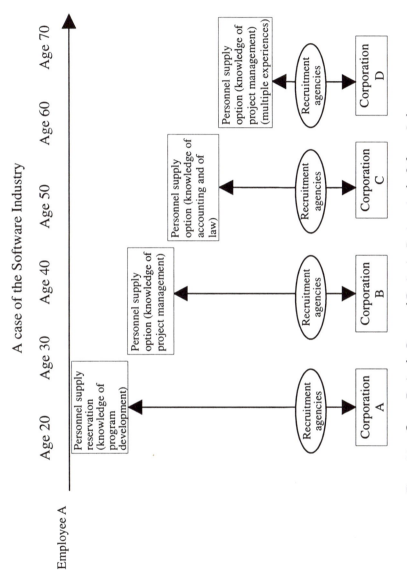

A case of the Software Industry

Employee A

Age 20   Age 30   Age 40   Age 50   Age 60   Age 70

Personnel supply reservation (knowledge of program development)

Personnel supply option (knowledge of project management)

Personnel supply option (knowledge of accounting and of law)

Personnel supply option (knowledge of project management) (multiple experiences)

Recruitment agencies

Corporation A

Recruitment agencies

Corporation B

Recruitment agencies

Corporation C

Recruitment agencies

Corporation D

Figure 21: Career Design by Personnel Derivative Business in the Software Industry

necessary knowledge, too. If there is a downturn in business they can withdraw their option rights.

Of course, it is possible for each individual employee to contract with companies directly. However, this is risky for corporations as it is difficult to judge if the employee has acquired the necessary knowledge by the time of the project. Therefore, it makes more sense if recruitment agencies manage contracts for groups of applicants.

As for the SDF reserve, there is a further auxiliary system called "Assistant Reserve System". When applicants pass the entrance examination and go through training (such as combat training) in the three year period in the free time they have while being engaged in other jobs, they will receive the total sum of 395,000 JPY, and they are entitled to become SDF reserve personnel after completing the training even if they are not retired SDF personnel. This system was started in 2002 and has been reported to have proven extremely popular, with applications running at six times the number of positions available.[5]

---

[5] "Young Applicants Swarming to Entrance Examination of SDF Assistant Reserve," Yomiuri Online, 14 April 2002 (http://www.yomiuri.co.jp/04/20020413i111.htm).

Chapter 4

Securing the Time Cost of Knowledge Transfer

4.1 The Current Situation

It takes time to understand and practice knowledge. However, most people lead busy lives, having little time for learning new knowledge. Currently, many companies are attempting to restructure by reducing personnel, which necessitates the remaining personnel to cover the extra workload by working longer hours. This deprives the employees of their opportunities to develop their skills, eventually lowering liquidity in the labor market.

4.2 Solutions

In this section, we will propose work-sharing as a measure to secure the time cost of knowledge transfer, and demonstrate how work-sharing schemes can be utilized to create time for knowledge transfer.

1) *Work-sharing as a measure to secure knowledge transfer time*

Work-sharing means: "To share a certain amount of workload among many employees by shortening working hours to secure employment".[1] It has come to the attention of Japanese society as a means to ease employment insecurity, since there have been many

---

[1] Shinmura, Izuru, *et al.*, *Kojien*, Iwanami Shoten, 1998.

recent cases of cutbacks as the unemployment rate has hit record heights since World War II.

"Survey Report on Work-Sharing" by the then Ministry of Labor classifies work-sharing schemes into four patterns as shown in Table 18.[2] What is notable here is the Diversified Working Patterns Type, which can be used as a measure to manage knowledge selection risks.

The Netherlands suffered a long-term recession as a result of the two oil crises since the 1970s, and the government has attempted major changes to the tax system, social security system, and labor law since 1982. The main changes include equal treatment of full-time and part-time workers and strict limitations on layoffs or dismissal — full-time and part-time workers were granted equal treatment and equal payment per hour for the same jobs, and companies were forced to obtain the regulator's permission and to present written documents regarding the grounds of dismissal before discharging employees. The success of these changes resulted in a decrease in the unemployment rate, which fell to less than 3%, and the national fiscal budget expenditure has turned positive for the first time in 25 years in 2000.

The Netherlands created a large number of part-time jobs through work-sharing, forming a work environment with values completely different from that of Japan. With the government's policies enforcing more strict rules on dismissal and promoting a shift from full-time to part-time work, employees were enabled to choose working hours that suited their lifestyle, and companies to control employment more smoothly.

Work-sharing can also be considered as a means to secure knowledge transfer time, as the extra free time created by work-sharing can be allocated to acquiring new knowledge. Although work-sharing is commonly regarded as a measure to create jobs for blue-collar workers, sharing menial labor, it has been put to

---

[2] Mitsui Knowledge Industry, Research Institute, commissioned by the then Ministry of Labor, "Survey Report on Work-Sharing," April 2001.

Table 18: Patterns of Work-Sharing and Examples of Cases

Patterns	Purpose	Cases of Implementation
Emergency Measure Type	Shorten the working hours of each employee to secure employment for the whole company as an emergency measure to survive temporary recession	Outside Japan, companies issue various benefits to alleviate loss of wage from the shortening of working hours. In Japan, there have been cases in which employees received lower wage as a result of this measure. Some companies limit the number of employees who are affected to lessen the objection from employees
Measure Aimed at Middle-Aged and Elderly Workers Type	Shorten the working hours of each employee to procure more jobs to secure employment for middle-aged and elderly employees	Measures to secure employment for employees over 60 (delayed retirement age and reemployment, etc.) in Japan
Job Creation Type	Shorten the working hours at corporate or national level to create new job openings for the unemployed	In European countries, governments grant benefits to alleviate the burden of companies and employees. Some companies shorten the working hours of elderly workers to create jobs for young workers
Diversified Working Patterns Type	Diversify working patterns of permanent employees to create more job opportunities for more employees including women and elderly workers	In the Netherlands, equal treatment for part-time workers was granted by a tripartite agreement, greatly promoting part-time jobs. Job sharing is another example of attempts in this category in other countries

use for white-collar workers, too. At Hewlett Packard, workers are allowed to share a workload that is normally for one employee between two, one employee working in the mornings, the other in the evenings, or one on certain days and the other the rest of the week. Applicants can choose their own partners, and they will be assessed in pairs for performance and promotion. Sun Microsystems has similar schemes.

There are still unresolved issues, such as how much lower wages resulting from the shortened working hours employees can accept, or how far work can be shared when the area of responsibility is unclear. It is, however, a concrete measure against knowledge obsolescence to secure the necessary study time for acquiring new knowledge.

2) *Diversified Working Patterns Type work-sharing*
   (new lifestyles in the Netherlands)

In the Netherlands, where Diversified Working Patterns Type work-sharing has been successfully introduced, various new lifestyles have appeared. According to Toshihisa Nagasaka, there are three working types: "Full-time with two days off, 36–38 working hours", "part-time with three days off, 30–32 working hours", and "half-time with half a week off, 20 working hours". Employees can select the working types that suit their situation (children, activities, study, etc.) and shift to different patterns if there is change in their lives.

The national government of the Netherlands recommends a "1.5 model" for couples (see Figure 22). Say if the husband works in an office and the wife does the house work, it is 1.0, and if both husband and wife work, it is 2.0. They recommend husband and wife working 1.5 in total as a couple. However, it has been pointed out that even in the Netherlands today, it is only a percentage of relatively young workers in the service industry in the cities who have managed the 1.5 model.[3]

---

[3]"The Actual Conditions of the Netherlands Model," (http://www.roumuya.net/zakkan/zakkan13/dutch.html).

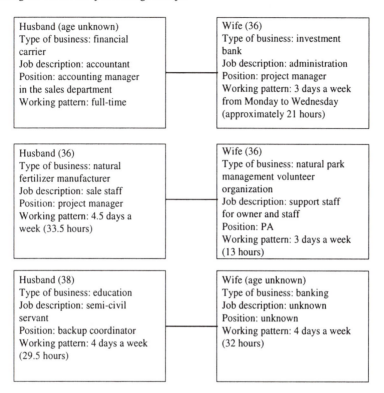

Figure 22:   Examples of Couples' Working Patterns in The Netherlands[4]

3)   *Securing time cost by work-sharing schemes*

Some kinds of knowledge require a considerable amount of time to acquire. Most companies offer paid leave, but taking a few months off is not practical as paid leave is not inexhaustible. Figure 23 demonstrates how a variant of work-sharing schemes enables employees to secure a block of time for knowledge transfer. For example, Tanaka does Task A full-time, and can use up the leave from Task A period during the period of Task B. This lowers the income, but it allows employees to secure both free time and the present employment.

---

[4]"Couples in Work-Sharing Advanced Country, The Netherlands," *Travaille*, 16 January 2001, No. 3.

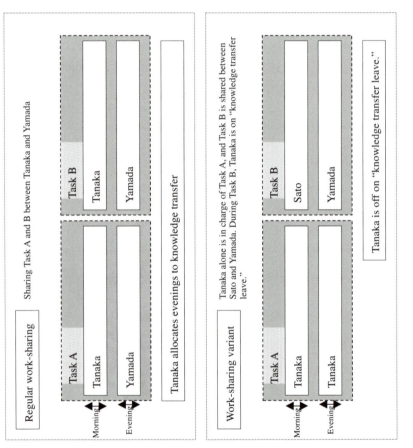

Figure 23:　An Example of the Utility of Work-Sharing for Knowledge Transfer

4) *Work-sharing in Japan*

Tables 19 and 20 show cases of work-sharing in Japanese organizations.

Fujitsu did extensive studies of introducing work-sharing schemes in the semiconductor sector for securing employment during the recession.[5] It was decided in the spring offensive of 2002 to change the shift work system from 2 shifts among 4 teams to 3 shifts among 6 teams, and to reduce the working hours of one shift from 12 to 8 h for the period of 3 months.[6] They further discussed a long-term leave system, although they decided not to introduce it that time. Individual workers could choose when they took leave, and they

Table 19: Companies Implementing or Discussing Work-Sharing

Prefectures	Content	Type
Hino Motors[7]	Implemented for 10 months since June 1999. Shortened the working hours of white-collar workers over age 55 except management (approximately 250 workers) by 1 h from 8 to 7 hours, and cut down wage including bonus by 10%	Emergency Measure Type
Fujitsu	Revision of shift work system and consideration of introducing mid-term leave in semiconductor factories	Emergency Measure Type
Sanyo Electric Co Ltd[8]	Would implement work-sharing scheme on 30,000 employees of 3 major companies of Sanyo Group in April 2002. Its period would be from 6 months to 3 years, with no cut down on hourly rate, and with limited wage loss	Emergency Measure Type

[5] "Long-term Leave, Fujistu," *Nihon Keizai Shimbun*, 9 January 2002.
[6] "Fujitsu: Management and Union Agree on Work-Sharing," *Nihon Keizai Shimbun*, 14 March 2002.
[7] "Actual Condition of Work-Sharing in a Certain Automobile Company," (http://www.mainichi.co.jp/life/family/shuppan/sunday/01/1125/tokushu1.html).
[8] "Sanyo to Introduce Work-Sharing Schemes," *Nihon Keizai Shimbun*, 19 December 2001.

Table 19:   (*Continued*)

Prefectures	Content	Type
Sharp Corporation[9]	In Fukuyama semiconductor factory, work-sharing has been introduced from January to March 2002. Shifts were increased from 2 to 3 shifts a day, which reduced 150 working hours in total per employee. Wage was not reduced but night duty pay was, successfully managing a 5% payroll cost reduction. Full-scale work-sharing would be discussed between the company and the employees	Emergency Measure Type

could allocate the time to acquiring new knowledge or to a side business. Wages during the long-term leave were reported to be much lower than standard layoff benefits.

The semiconductor industry fluctuates greatly according to changes in the economy, and companies are exploring options to secure employees and to cut down on payroll costs at the same time by shortening working hours. This system can be categorized as a

Table 20:   Prefectures Implementing or Discussing Work-Sharing

Corporations	Content	Type
Hyogo[10]	Cut down on overwork pay in the governor's departments and agencies by 5% per year (approx. 200 million JPY) since 2000. Hired new and recent graduates for one year as contract part–time workers. Working hours were limited to 4 days a week (30 hours), and monthly wage was 155,000 JPY. Many young employees worked in the municipal office for a year, while studying for examinations and qualifications during days-off and night time	Job Creation Type

---

[9]"Sharp to Partially Introduce Work-Sharing Schemes," *Nihon Keizai Shimbun*, 11 January 2002.
[10]"Editorial," *To-o Nippo*, 19 December 2001.

Table 20:   (*Continued*)

Hokkaido[11]	Governor Tatsuya Hori announced the plan to hire 150 high school graduates under 20, funded by cut-down on civil servants' overtime work. In the initial budget for 2002, the municipal office's overtime work payment was 7% of the entire budget (approx. 4.7 billion JPY). Its 5% (230 million JPY) was secured for the scheme, for training and creating jobs for high school graduates, thus promoting them to be hired in the private sector	Job Creation Type
Aichi[12]	Aichi Management Association and Aichi Workers' Association agreed on basic ideas about work-sharing for securing employment (17 December 2001). They would notify member corporations and labor unions of their policies	Unknown
Fukushima[13]	"Prefectural Work-Sharing Discussion Panel", composed of the municipal government, representatives of labor union and representatives of management, was established. Its first meeting was held on 25 January 2002. They would hold seven meetings in total and would publish a report	Unknown

kind of employment reservation, in that employees will be restored to employment preferentially once the economy recovers.

As for municipal governments, Hyogo Prefecture has been actively exploring the possibilities of work-sharing schemes (see Table 21). Hyogo Labor Union, Hyogo Management Association and the municipal government of Hyogo agreed to cooperate in implementing work-sharing schemes in Hyogo Prefecture in December 1999. They announced "Work-Sharing Guidelines"

---

[11] "The Hokkaido Municipal Office to Introduce Work-Sharing Schemes," *Mainichi Shimbun (Hokkaido Prefecture Edition)*, 5 January 2002.
[12] Business@nifty, 7 December 2001 (http://business.nifty.com/news2/te/ 20011207 te020.htm).
[13] Fukushima News (http://headlines.yahoo.co.jp/hl?a=20020126-00000006-mai-l07).

Table 21:   The Chronology of Work-Sharing in Hyogo Prefecture

Dates	Efforts
6 June 1999	"Employment Measure Tripartite Council" was established (Hyogo Labor Union, Hyogo Management Association and the municipal government)
16 August 1999	The council announced "Job Creation Tripartite Declaration" and "Secure Employment, Job Creation Plan", including work-sharing guidelines by employees and management
17 December 1999	The council announced "Agreement on Hyogo Type Work-Sharing"
1 February 2000	"Work-Sharing Committee" was launched, consisted of Hyogo Labor Union and Hyogo Management Association). Meetings were held four times until 27 March 2000
29 May 2000	Hyogo Labor Union and Hyogo Management Association formed "Work-Sharing Guidelines"
18 July 2000	"Work-Sharing Hyogo Symposium" was held by Hyogo Labor Union, Hyogo Management Association and the municipal government
11 September 2000	"Work-Sharing Advisor Service" was launched by the municipal government
4 October 2000	"Work-Sharing Promotion Exchange" was held by Hyogo Labor Union and Hyogo Management Association three times until 8 December 2000
30 January 2001	"Work-Sharing International Symposium" was held by Hyogo Labor Union, Hyogo Management Association and the municipal government
1 April 2001	"Diversified Working Patterns Study Group" was formed by the municipal government
1 July 2001	Survey on Hyogo Type work-sharing
27 December 2001	"Work-Sharing Model" was commenced by the municipal government

Source: "The Chronology of Work-Sharing in Hyogo Prefecture," (http://web. pref.hyogo.jp/koyou/worksharing/wshistr.htm).

on 29 May 2000. A "Work-Sharing Advisor Service" was launched in September 2000, dispatching advisors on work-sharing implementation for free (up to 8 h). A "Work-Sharing Introduction Model" was commenced in December 2001, providing up to one million JPY to companies when work-sharing schemes are introduced.

5)   *Various situations of work-sharing in different countries*

Most work-sharing schemes in Japan are of the Emergency Measure Type, but as in Germany, Job Creation Type work-sharing can be used as a measure to promote a transition of power between generations by encouraging the early retirement of elderly workers, or as in the Netherlands, it can be used as a measure to improve the quality of life or to enable diversified working patterns (see Table 22). Its full potential would be left unexplored if it was only considered as an employment policy.

There are many problems to be solved before work-sharing can be implemented. For example, how to divide workload, how to evaluate employees, how to deal with employees whose wages are affected by work-sharing, how to deal with employees' side businesses, and so on.

Table 22:   Work-Sharing in the World

Countries	Schemes
France	35 h labor law The national benefit system (An employee is entitled to the government's benefits if he spontaneously shortens his working hours by 50%)
Germany	Creating jobs for younger generations by elderly workers' early retirement
The Netherlands	Part-time employment (NB: section 2)
Sweden	Free Year System (An employee is entitled to 3 months to 1 year leave, if he has been engaged in the job for more than 2 years)

Source: Hokkaido Prefecture, "Work-Sharing Field Survey," September 2000.

Currently the work-sharing schemes adopted in Japanese companies are antirecession measures, but if the roles of employees and companies become clearer through discussion of work-sharing, it can be a very effective tool to reassess the sharing of knowledge selection risks in the employee–company relationship.

Chapter 5

Improving the Efficiency of Knowledge Transfer Systems

5.1 The Current Situation

Even if sufficient time for knowledge transfer is secured, if the transfer system is inefficient, the success rate is low. For example, a lecture produces uneven results depending on the quality of the lecturer and the students. However, high efficiency and high return are desirable.

Another factor to consider is that the opportunity for knowledge transfer may be limited if the transfer system can only be offered in certain places or at certain times. These restrictions may cause an uneven distribution of knowledge among candidates for knowledge transfer.

5.2 Solutions

To improve the efficiency of knowledge transfer, we should: (1) develop educational methods, and (2) correct the uneven distribution of transfer opportunities.

1) Developments in educational methods

Teaching materials with various devices to improve learning efficiency have recently been produced. For example, software which combines typing practice and vocabulary building for words frequently used in TOEIC,[1] and multimedia language learning software.[2]

The former software displays the definitions of words on screen, prompting users to type in the words, with the pronunciations read out from the speaker. If the users type the words correctly, loud sound effects congratulate him and prompt him to study further.

The latter software contains video clips for each conversation exercise, allowing users to learn the phrases used in actual scenes. On the back of advances in IT technologies, more of these innovations are expected to follow.

In October 1998, Aoyama Gakuin University launched the Aoyama Media Lab (AML) project, with the aim of establishing new educational methods and constructing a cyber campus (see Figure 24). AML consists of a Management and Technology Integration Strategy IT Study Group, a Cyber Campus Educational Method Development Project, and an AML Consortium.[3]

The Management and Technology Integration Strategy IT Study Group, which includes domestic and international educational institutions, public organizations and corporations, is engaged in the research of new management strategies based on IT innovations, and on the IT to put them into practice.

The Cyber Campus Educational Method Development Project is engaged in the development of programs, teaching materials, educational software, and the testing of their validity in demonstration classes, with the aim of using them in regular university classes. It also conducts development and management of the environment for educational systems (i.e., educational institutions, equipment and materials to support new educational methods) and amassing of management know-how, and attempts to reduce the investment risk for partner educational institutions and corporations. The AML

---

[1]Tokutan by Sourcenext, K. K.
[2]ENCARTA by Microsoft.
[3]"About AML," (http://am12.a2en.aoyama.ac.jp/contents2_katsudou.shtml).

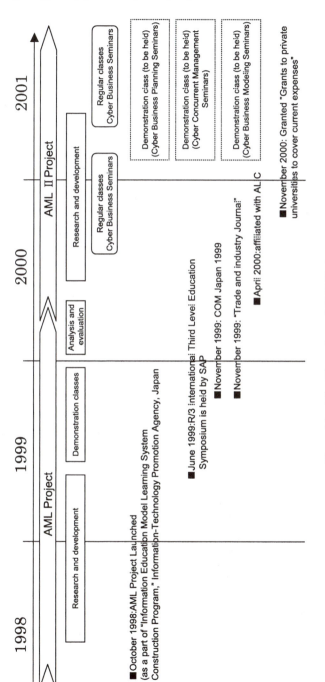

Figure 24: The Chronology of AML Project

Consortium publishes and promotes the research developments of the project.

These innovations and the research are expected to make further progress. When various learning devices and methods are developed and users are able to select the ones that suit them best, individuals can try to improve their learning efficiency according to their preferences and thus lessen knowledge transfer risk.

2) *Correcting the uneven distribution of study opportunities*

The development of network technology produced e-learning. E-learning enables learners to study in their own time and location by providing them with lessons and learning materials via the Internet. It also enables learners to participate in the classes of famous lecturers. More and more major American corporations have started to introduce e-learning through their training management systems that incorporate personnel management and that measure the efficiency and performance of employees' training plans (see Figure 25).

Nova Corporation, which is a major language school company in Japan, started an online 24-hour lesson service. Also, numerous postgraduate schools for working people were launched, offering courses both during the day and in the evening. A certain course allows students to obtain MBAs from American universities without

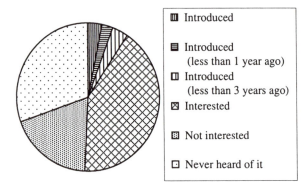

Figure 25:   Companies that Introduced E-Learning
Source: "Review: 2001," *Nikkan Kogyo Shimbun* (*Daily Industrial*), 19 December 2001.

actually going to America; students can take the course via satellite TV and obtain an MBA on the successful completion of the course.

The Massachusetts Institute of Technology (MIT) is broadcasting all its lectures on the Internet, allowing students from all over the world to participate.[4] Stanford University has started distributing lectures on some courses, for example production control, to Hitachi Ltd and Toyota Motor Corporation since 2002. A university official noted, "Setting up a campus in Japan would be too costly but an online campus is not". The Information Engineering Department of Shinshu University, Nagano, Japan, launched an Internet graduate program in 2002, which enables students to obtain master's degrees through online lectures.[5]

Daiwa Securities Co Ltd has announced that they have adopted an online training system for all employees.[6] The system distributes texts on approximately 2000 topics relating to products and taxation that are necessary for the employees via the Internet, so that employees can download and study the texts.

Further improvements would guarantee e-learning as an effective tool to correct the uneven distribution of study opportunities, resulting from restrictions on time and place.

---

[4]"MIT to Make Nearly All Course Materials Available Free on the World Wide Web," (http://web.mit.edu/newsoffice/nr/2001/ocw.html).
[5]http://www.cs.shinshu-u.ac.jp/Nyushi/sugsi/sugsipress.html
[6]Yomiuri Online, 14 April 2002 (http://www.yomiuri.co.jp/02/20020414ib01.htm).

Chapter 6

The Framework of Knowledge Selection Society

Major Japanese companies used to play various roles in Japanese society. While pursuing their own profits and market share, they maintained employment, provided each employee with training opportunities, a sense of security and of belonging and job satisfaction, and even considered their career planning too. This was no mean feat. Nonetheless, the motivating premise behind these roles is disappearing.

With the shortening of knowledge life, a knowledge selection society is emerging, where people come across knowledge selection opportunities many times. Because of knowledge obsolescence, everyone will have the bitter experience of losing a hard-earned career position. This will not be a unique occurrence caused by the individual's fault. In fact, this will happen to everyone.

Under these circumstances, it is vital that everyone is allowed to attempt something new when the opportunity arises. For that reason, there must not be vested interests, and the balance of risk to be shared between employees and companies has to be revised so that knowledge selection risk can be alleviated when it manifests itself.

Furthermore, in a knowledge selection society, no one can predict for sure which knowledge will be advantageous; the only difference would be in the degree of confidence in the prediction. Therefore, companies should not impose their own choice of new knowledge on their employees. Employees should conduct knowledge selection according to their plan of further educating themselves. To alleviate the burden on employees, supply/demand information of knowledge

Figure 26:   The Framework of a Knowledge Selection Society

should be made available, and knowledge selection risk management systems should be established, which control selection risks intelligently according to the circumstances.

Figure 26 illustrates major players in alleviating knowledge selection risk.

It cannot be only companies that will bear the task of alleviating knowledge selection risk as before, but it would be too much of a burden on employees alone. We need new institutions and systems to allocate and share knowledge selection risks between companies and individual workers in a knowledge selection society.

The formation of a knowledge market is essential for society to share knowledge selection risk. This market will also be a trading place for human resources. For this market to be established, knowledge standardization institutions that provide people with options in knowledge selection, and also educational institutions that offer effective knowledge transfer, will have to be fully developed. Information on knowledge supply/demand and education will have to be distributed and shared among people. Finally, there should be advisors for the evaluation of the shared information, for personnel supply and career design, and for the alleviation of knowledge selection risk.

It may be that in future, each individual will have a personal manager, just like in show-business, giving advice on marketing, career planning and selection of jobs.

Summary

People who are concerned with knowledge can be divided into creators and practitioners. The former might appear valuable from the point of view of their contribution to the entire human civilization's wealth of wisdom, but the latter are essential in practical terms.

Exploring how knowledge selection risk should be shared in society means creating a system that will produce knowledge practitioners efficiently.

Japan had successful models in foreign corporations and industries when the country was planning the reconstruction of industries after World War II. With the government's thorough protection policies, Japanese companies had only to copy successful cases of knowledge transfer in other countries. When the national economy was growing rapidly, Japanese companies did not have to face large-scale knowledge selection, which might have jeopardized their already amassed knowledge, as the main focus was on securing stable business relationships. Although knowledge selection on a small scale did frequently take place, knowledge selection risk did not come to the surface, as it was absorbed by corporate efforts like diversification. Labor supply was scarce because of the rapid expansion of business. Therefore, the life employment and seniority-based pay systems were suitable for Japanese corporations in this era.

However, the premises for these systems were overthrown by the stagnating economy and the shortening of knowledge lifespan. Without smooth knowledge transfer, obsolete knowledge and its practitioners will be accumulated in companies as unprofitable assets.

Maintaining lifetime employment or seniority-based pay systems in this new age would be the same as asking the employees to carry out a suicide pact with obsolete knowledge.

We have argued that knowledge practitioners are crucial to knowledge transfer, and that people are exposed to knowledge selection risk as knowledge lifespan is becoming increasingly shorter. Existing systems cannot alleviate or cover this risk sufficiently. The obsolescence of knowledge does not allow corporations and employees to live comfortably in the existing systems. The risk is too much for companies to bear on their own, but it is also impossible for individuals alone to do so. Both companies and individual workers will have to respond to this change in society, build up new systems, and establish new courses of action.

In the second part of this book, we suggested ideas for managing knowledge selection risk. Personnel supply derivative contracts will be a new tool for matching supply and demand in the labor market. The suggestions vary from those that can be tried out locally with the existing IT technology, to those that need drastic legal reform. We hope that our suggestions are helpful in facing the change in the environment.

Finally, we would like to thank Isao Higashihara and Takayuki Toyama, instructors, Tokyo Denki University; Toshio Akimoto, associate professor, Toyo University; Tomoaki Fujimori, professor at Chiba Keizai University; Hidehisa Shibata, associate lecturer at the Research Center for Advanced Science and Technology, University of Tokyo; Masafumi Kotani, IBM Japan; Toshinari Chinen, Johnson & Johnson; and Hiroko Suetake, Graduate School of Business Administration, Meiji University, for their advice.

Appendix

Positioning Analysis of Vendors Based on Customer Satisfaction Survey of "Application Related Service" Industry

A.1   Purpose

The result for the "Sixth Survey on Computer Customer Satisfaction" was published in *Nikkei Computer* on 18 December 2000. This survey was conducted among 7812 medium-sized leading firms, on customer satisfaction for system development vendors (hereafter called "vendors"). It covered 18 areas, including "servers", "office computers" and "mainframe computers", among which "application related services" produced rather interesting results. Particular companies scored high points even though there were no less than 12 questions. The competition in this industry was said to be fierce since famous vendors such as NEC or Hitachi entered it, but as the survey shows, a certain order seems to have already been formed.

This report attempts to discover fundamental factors forming the order of the vendors, based on the questions of customer satisfaction survey.

A.2   Method of Analysis

1)   *Objectives*

We used the results for "application related service" section of the "Sixth Survey on Computer Customer Satisfaction," which was published in *Nikkei Computer*.[1] This is an annual survey of system departments of medium-sized leading firms.

This year, system departments of 7812 firms were surveyed.[2] Questionnaires were sent out on 4 October 2000, and answers that were sent back by 19 October 2000 were tallied. 1980 firms sent valid answers, which made the total rate of collection 25.3%.

There were questions in various items about products and service. System departments would choose their answers out of four options: (1) Dissatisfied, (2) Rather dissatisfied, (3) Rather satisfied, and (4) Satisfied. Points were given to each answer: (1) 0 point, (2) 33.3 points, (3) 66.7 points, and (4) 100 points, respectively. Finally, points were tallied for each article for each vendor. Since the data published in *Nikkei Computer* was already translated into points, we used this data in our analysis.

2)   Analysis data

The data for analysis is shown in Table 23. The shaded figures are the highest and second highest scores in each section. This shows that a small group of firms including IBM Japan dominates the high rankings.

3)   Analysis method

We used factor analysis to determine if there were fundamental factors behind the sections of customer satisfaction survey.

---

[1] "Application related service" here refers to planning and development of applications for core corporate functions and information analysis, and does not include mere installation support. It mainly denotes development of applications, specially fitted to the nature of each firm's business.

[2] Companies listed on the first and second sections of the Tokyo Stock Exchange, and on the JASDAQ Market, or listed firms with annual turnover of more than 20 billion JPY.

Table 23: Data for Analysis

Names of Corporations	Speed of Development	Meeting the Deadlines	Meeting the Budget	Planning	Work Analysis	Skills	Project Management	Response to Specification Changes	Quality of Final Products	Initial Response to Problems	Trouble Shooting	Service Fees
IBM Japan	65	67	61	67	66	77	65	59	68	66	66	36
Nihon Unisys	61	70	68	59	65	67	63	63	67	69	65	46
Hitachi	60	63	63	53	56	69	57	59	63	64	62	46
NEC	58	61	62	52	52	64	53	54	59	58	56	45
Fujitsu	57	59	61	54	54	64	55	54	58	56	55	44
Oki Electric Industry	58	70	73	50	61	58	51	67	65	61	67	47
Toshiba	52	63	54	45	43	57	52	43	52	54	52	36
NCR Japan	48	59	61	47	48	54	50	44	58	61	59	35
NTT	61	72	69	62	60	69	61	64	68	69	67	48
NTT Data	58	66	62	61	64	70	59	55	59	60	60	39
NEC Software	58	60	64	46	49	62	51	58	55	61	56	45
Fujitsu Business Systems Japan	56	53	65	45	49	57	46	53	55	55	50	43
CSK	68	71	65	57	57	65	58	54	61	61	61	42

	1	2	3	4	5
Eigenvalue	7.7811	2.0727	0.7673	0.3765	0.2731
Difference	5.7083	1.3054	0.3908	0.1034	0.1533
Proportion	0.6799	0.1811	0.0670	0.0329	0.0239
Cumulative	0.6799	0.8611	0.9281	0.9610	0.9849

	6	7	8	9	10
Eigenvalue	0.1198	0.0565	0.0452	0.0087	-0.0010
Difference	0.0633	0.0113	0.0365	0.0097	0.0213
Proportion	0.0105	0.0049	0.0039	0.0008	-0.0001
Cumulative	0.9953	1.0003	1.0042	1.0050	1.0049

	11	12
Eigenvalue	-0.0223	-0.0338
Difference	0.0115	
Proportion	-0.0019	-0.0030
Cumulative	1.0030	1.0000

Figure 27:   Eigenvalues and Cumulatives

A.3   Results and Conclusions

1)   *Determination of the factors*

Eigenvalues of each factor, difference of eigenvalues, proportions and cumulatives are shown in Figure 27. The cumulative of the first factor reaches approximately 68%, and that of the second approximately 86%. The eigenvalues of factors later than the third were less than 1. Therefore, we used the first and second factors in this analysis.

2)   *Factor loadings and final communality*

The factor loadings and the final communality of this factor analysis are shown in Figure 28. The final communality reaches 9.853809. Therefore, we conclude that factor space is highly accounted for. We used the varimax rotation method.

3)   *Interpretation of factors*

The first factor shows high correlation for "project management", "planning", "skills", "work analysis", "quality of final products", "initial response to problems", "meeting the deadlines", and "speed

	FACTOR1	FACTOR2	
X7	0.97378	-0.01349	Project management
X4	0.97019	0.02227	Planning
X6	0.89431	-0.00308	Skills
X5	0.85791	0.35390	Work analysis
X9	0.79582	0.50655	Quality of final products
X11	0.75342	0.49960	Trouble shooting
X10	0.73977	0.44350	Initial response to problems
X2	0.71537	0.39072	Meeting the deadlines
X1	0.69536	0.29496	Speed of development
X3	0.16931	0.95680	Meeting the budget
X12	-0.02929	0.87331	Service fees
X8	0.47450	0.82686	Response to specification changes

Variance explained by each factor

FACTOR1	FACTOR2
6.423491	3.430319

Final Communality Estimates: Total = 9.853809

Figure 28: Rotated Factor Loadings and Final Communality

of development".[3] The second factor, on the other hand, shows high correlation to "quality of final products", "meeting the budget", "service fees", and "response to specification changes".

We surmise from this that while the first factor demonstrates the "performance" of vendors, the second factor demonstrates the "sincerity" of vendors that customers sensed from their service. Vendors who would meet the budget and respond to specification changes are good, sincere vendors. In that sense, the second factor can be regarded as "sincerity in accommodating to customers' demands".

The positioning of vendors for the first and second factors is given in Figure 29.

Figure 29 is quite interesting. The vertical axis is the first factor, which can be interpreted as "technical performance"; IBM Japan is

---

[3]"High correlation" is defined here as those whose absolute values of correlation are over 0.5.

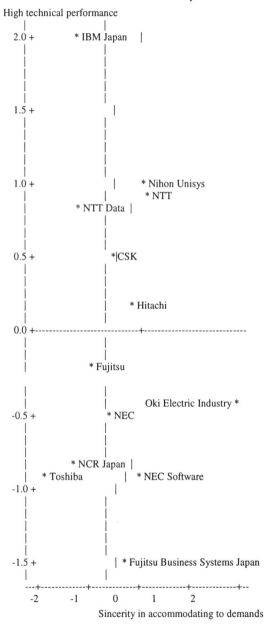

Figure 29:   The Positioning of Vendors for the First and Second Factors

outstanding, with Nihon Unisys, NTT and NTT Data following. The horizontal axis is the second factor, which can be interpreted as "sincerity in accommodating to customers' demands"; IBM Japan falls behind traditional Japanese firms such as Oki Electric Industry, NTT and Hitachi.

This means that even though IBM Japan wins high acclaim for its "technical performance", it has a low reputation for "sincerity". It may be that they tend to neglect customers' special requests on the back of their high technology. Nihon Unisys and NTT are well-balanced in these two factors, although they do not possess technology as advanced as that of IBM Japan.

The customer satisfaction survey has 12 points of evaluation, each of which represents each stage in application related service, such as planning, development and management.

This analysis shows that customers do not place an emphasis on any one single stage; for them, "technical performance" and "sincerity" are the main criteria for evaluating vendors.

References

[1] "Sixth Survey on Computer Customer Satisfaction," *Nikkei Computer*, 18 December 2000.
[2] Saito, Masahiko, *Introduction to Linear Algebra*, Tokyo University Press, 1995.
[3] Asano, Hirohiko, *Introduction to Practical Multivariate Analysis*, Kodansha, 1996.

Bibliography

Books

Aoki, Masahiko, *et al.*, *The Role of the Market, The Role of the State*, Toyo Keizai, 1999.

Arthur Andersen Consulting, *Leveraging Corporate Competency with Knowledge Management*, Toyo Keizai, 1999.

Asano, Hirohiko, *Introduction to Practical Multivariate Analysis*, Kodansha, 1996.

Burton-Jones, Alan, *Knowledge Capitalism* (translation of the original *Knowledge Capitalism: Business, Work, and Learning in the New Economy* in English), Nihon Keizai Shimbun, 2001.

Career Development Center, *Corporate Groups and Industrial Maps*, Takahashi Shoten, 2001.

Christensen, Clayton M., *Dilemma in Innovation* (translation of the original *The Innovator's Dilemma: When New Technologies Cause Great Firms to Fall* in English), Shoeisha, 2000.

Drucker, P. F., *Innovation and Entrepreneurship* (translation of the original *Innovation and Entrepreneurship* in English), Diamond, 1997.

Drucker, P. F., *The Requirements for Professionals* (translation of the original *Post-Capitalist Society* in English), Diamond, 2000.

Drucker, P. F., *et al.*, *Knowledge Management* (translation of the original *Harvard Business Review on Knowledge Management* in English), Diamond, 2000.

Gause, Donald C. and Gerald M. Weinberg, *Exploring Requirements* (translation of the original *Exploring Requirements: Quality Before Design* in English), Kyoritsu Shuppan, 1993.

GE Corporate Executive Office, *The Jack Welch Years at GE*, Diamond, 2001.

Hanada, Mitsuyo, *et al.*, *Paradigm Change in Career Designing*, Diamond, 1995.

Hatano, Giyoo (Ed.), *Cognitive Psychology 5: Study and Development*, Tokyo University Press, 1996.

Hull, John C., *Financial Engineering Third Edition* (translation of the original *Options, Futures, and other Derivatives* in English), Kinzai Institute for Financial Affairs, 1998.

Information Processing Society of Japan (Ed.), *Knowledge Engineering*, Ohmsha, 1987.

Introduction to Derivatives, Ginko Kenshusha, 1995.

Ishikawa, Akira, *et al.*, *Cybernetics Renaissance*, Kogyo Chosakai Publishing, 1999.

Japan Almanac 2002, Asahi Shimbun, 2001.

Japan Information Processing Development Corporation (Ed.), *White Paper on Informatization*, Computer Age, 2001.

Komiya, Ryutaro, *Industrial Policies in Japan*, Tokyo University Press, 1984.

Komiya, Ryutaro, *The Japanese Economy: Trade, Industry, and Government*, Tokyo University Press, 1991.

Konno, Noboru, *Knowledge Asset Management*, Nihon Keizai Shimbun, 1998.
Konno, Noboru, *Management of Intellectual Property*, Nihon Keizai Shimbun, 1998.
Kuwata, Kotaro and Masao Tao, *Organizations*, Yuhikaku Arma, 1998.
Leonard, Dorothy, *Wellsprings of Knowledge* (translation of the original *Wellsprings of Knowledge: Building and Sustaining the Sources of Innovation* in English), Diamond, 2001.
Maeda, Takeshi and Fumio Aoki, *New Artificial Intelligence*, Ohmsha, 1999.
Miura, Kazuo and Toki Ura, *How to Create a Temporary Staffing Company*, Pal Publishing, 1999.
Morinaga, Takuro, *Corporate Restructuring and Merit System*, Kodansha, 2000.
Muta, Seiichiro, *Interest-Rate Options*, Kindai Sales, 1995.
Nagasaka, Toshihisa, *Dutch Model*, Nihon Keizai Shimbun, 2000.
Nakajima, Yoshiaki, *et al.* (Eds.), *The Yuhikaku Dictionary of Psychology*, Yuhikaku, 1999.
Nishimura, Katsumi, *Introduction of IT to Medium and Small Firms*, X-Media, 2001.
Nishio, Shojiro, *Database*, Ohmsha, 2000.
Noguchi, Yukio, *Farewell, Wartime Economy*, Toyo Keizai, 1995.
Nonaka, Ikujiro and Hirotaka Takeuchi, *The Knowledge-Creating Company*, Toyo Keizai, 1996.
Oe, Ken, *Why New Enterprises Do Not Succeed*, Nihon Keizai Shimbun, 1998.
Outsourcing and Evolution of Organizations, Diamond, 1996.
Porter, Michael E. and Hirotaka Takeuchi, *Can Japan Compete?* (in Japanese), Diamond, 2000.
Reich, Robert B., *The Work of Nations* (translation of the original *The Work of Nations: Preparing Ourselves for 21st-Century Capitalism* in English), Diamond, 1991.
Saito, Masahiko, *Introduction to Linear Algebra*, Tokyo University Press, 1995.
Shibata, Hidetoshi and Tomohito Ihara, *Business Method Patents*, Toyo Keizai, 2000.
Shimamoto, Tadashi, *et al.*, *Perfect Guide to Constructing Web Service*, Nikkei Business Publications, 2001.
Shimizu, Takashi, *Mergers and Lifespan of Corporations*, Yuhikaku, 2001.
Shinmura, Izuru, *et al.*, *Kojien*, Iwanami Shoten, 1998.
Shiozawa, Minobu, *Comparison of Japanese Companies: Publishers*, Jitsumukyoiku-Shuppan, 2001.
Suematsu, Chihiro, *How the Net Changes the Whole Financial Industry*, Diamond, 1999.
Tissen, Rene, Daniel Andriessen, and Frank Lopez, *Value-Based Knowledge Management* (translation of the original *The Knowledge Dividend: Creating High-Performance Companies through Value-Based Knowledge Management* in English), Pearson Education, 2000.
Ueki, Masahiro, *Derivative Documentation*, Kindai Sales, 1995.
Weinberg, Gerald M., *Secrets of Consulting* (translation of the original *Secrets of Consulting: A Guide to Giving and Getting Advice Successfully* in English), Kyoritsu Shuppan, 1990.
Weinberg, Gerald M., *Becoming a Super Engineer* (translation of the original *Becoming a Technical Leader: An Organic Problem-Solving Approach* in English), Kyoritsu Shuppan, 1991.
Wurman, Richard Saul, *Understanding Secrets* (translation of the original *Information Anxiety* in English), NTT Publishing, 1993.
Yoshida, Kazuo (Ed.), *The National Budget of Japan*, Kodansha, 1996.

Journal Articles

Aoyama, Mikio, "Introduction to Software Service Technology," *Information Processing*, September 2001, 42 (9): 857–862.
Hagiwara, Masayoshi, ".NET Framework," *Information Processing*, September 2001, 42 (9): 878–882.

Takase, Toshiro, "UDDI and WSDL," *Information Processing*, September 2001, 42 (9): 870–877.

Newspaper Articles/Other Periodicals

"20,000 Workers to Work on Preventing Cyber Terrorism," *Nihon Keizai Shimbun*, 24 December 2001.

"American Universities Having Lectures on Management in Japan," *Nihon Keizai Shimbun*, 15 January 2002.

"AMS Japan and Temp Staff Collaborate in IT Personnel Training," *Nihon Keizai Shimbun*, 6 January 2002.

"Can We Break the Vicious Circle?" *Nihon Keizai Shimbun*, 9 January 2002.

"Collaboration of Major IT Engineer Training Firms," *Nihon Keizai Shimbun*, 21 January 2002.

"Couples in Work-Sharing Advanced Country, The Netherlands," *Travaille*, 16 January 2001.

"Cross-Holding Shares of More than Five Trillion Yen Sold," *Nikkei Kinyu Shimbun*, 6 December 2001.

"DBM Japan to Join the Career Counselor Business," *Nihon Keizai Shimbun*, 3 January 2002.

"Discussion: Employment," *Nikkei Sangyo Shimbun*, 11 December 2001.

Drucker, P.F., "The Future of Management in the Twenty-First Century," *Weekly Diamond*, 27 November 1999.

"Early Retirement," *Nikkei Sangyo Shimbun*, 7 January 2002.

"Editorial," *To-o Nippo*, 19 December 2001.

"Employment Fault 2," *Nihon Keizai Shimbun*, 24 December 2001.

"Fierce Competition in the IT Service Industry," *Nihon Keizai Shimbun*, 3 November 2001.

"Fuji Xerox: Assessment of Employee Marketability," *Nikkei Sangyo Shimbun*, 1 April 2002.

"Fujitsu: Management and Union Agree on Work-Sharing," *Nihon Keizai Shimbun*, 14 March 2002.

"Fujitsu, Remodeling in Major Factories," *Nihon Keizai Shimbun*, 26 December 2001.

"Fujitsu to Introduce Long-term Leave," *Nihon Keizai Shimbun*, 9 January 2002.

"Hitachi, Toshiba, and other Electronics Manufacturers Set Up Training Courses," *Nihon Keizai Shimbun*, 2 January 2002.

"Long-term Leave, Fujitsu," *Nihon Keizai Shimbun*, 9 January 2002.

"National Airplanes to be Developed," *Nihon Keizai Shimbun*, 24 November 2001.

"NEC Internally Published Management Grade Responsibilities," *Nihon Keizai Shimbun*, 28 March 2002.

"Online Application to be Standardized in June," *Nihon Keizai Shimbun*, 12 April 2002.

"Online Temporary Staffing Business, Manpower," *Nikkei Sangyo Shimbun*, 28 January 2002.

"Powerful Ally of Busy Drinking and Eating Establishments, Fullcast: Registered Members 10,000," *Nihon Keizai Shimbun*, 1 April 2002.

"Review: 2001," *Nikkan Kogyo Shimbun (Daily Industrial)*, 19 December 2001.

"Sanyo to Introduce Work-Sharing Schemes," *Nihon Keizai Shimbun*, 19 December 2001.

"Sharp to Partially Introduce Work-Sharing Schemes," *Nihon Keizai Shimbun*, 11 January 2002.

"Sixth Survey on Computer Customer Satisfaction," *Nikkei Computer*, 18 December 2000.

"Temporary Staffing Firms Promote Mid-career Change," *Nihon Keizai Shimbun*, 28 January 2002.

"Temporary Staffing: Professional Career to be Expanded," *Nihon Keizai Shimbun*, 28 January 2002.

"The Dawn of Service-Oriented Era," *Nikkei Computer*, 5 November 2001.

"The Future of Server System," *Nikkei Computer*, 5 November 2001.

"The Hokkaido Municipal Office to Introduce Work-Sharing Schemes," *Mainichi Shimbun* (Hokkaido Prefecture Edition), 5 January 2002.

"Toshiba, Retreat from DRAM," *Nihon Keizai Shimbun*, 19 December 2001.

"Turning Point of Nuclear Power," *Nikkei Sangyo Shimbun*, July 2001.

"Viewpoint of Think-Tank: Memory is the Ultimate Customer Satisfaction," *Nikkan Kogyo Shimbun (Daily Industrial)*, 9 January 2002.

Reports/Surveys/Company Press Releases

Hitachi Ltd, "Financial Statement Report, Fiscal Year Ended 31 March 2001," 2001.

Hitachi News Releases, "Hitachi to Reconstruct its Semiconductor Business," 10 October 2001.

Hitachi News Releases, "Development of High-Performance Strained-Silicon-Transistor Technology," 6 December 2001.

Hitachi News Releases, "Hitachi and Mitsubishi to Cooperate on Basic Technologies," 20 February 2002.

Hokkaido Prefecture, "Work-Sharing Field Survey," September 2000.

Hyogo Management Association, Rengo (Japanese Trade Union Confederation), "Guideline for Work Sharing," May 2000.

Japan Federation of Economic Organizations, "Proposal for Tax Reform," 12 September 2000.

Japan Information Technology Promotion Agency, "The Standard for Information Technology Engineer Skills," January 2004.

Japan Institute of Labor, "Survey on Companies Utilizing IT and on the Labor Conditions in Information-Related Companies," 2001.

Japan Research Institute of Labor, "FY 2001 White Paper," 2001.

Management and Coordination Agency (Ed.), "White Paper on Deregulation, 2000," 2000.

Ministry of Finance, "Summary of Budget and Fiscal Investment and Loan Program Plan, FY 2001," 2001.

Ministry of Internal Affairs and Communications (Ed.), "Information and Communications in Japan, White Paper 2001," 2001.

Mitsui Knowledge Industry, Research Institute, commissioned by the then Ministry of Labor, "Survey Report on Work-Sharing," April 2001.

National Institute of Science and Technology Policy, "Assessment of the Effects of R&D Policy on Economic Growth," June 1999.

Personnel and Labor Management Study Group, "Research on Personnel Management and Training Investment in the Performance-Based Pay Era," 8 August 2000.

Study Committee on the Japanese Employment System, "Research on the Condition of Workers' Career Development and Awareness," June–August 1999.

Toshiba Press Releases, "Toshiba Announces Reorganization of Memory Business," 18 December 2001.

Online Resources

"About AML," (http://am12.a2en.aoyama.ac.jp/contents2_katsudon.shtml).

"Actual Condition of Work-Sharing in a Certain Automobile Company," (http://www.mainichi. co.jp/life/family/shuppan/sunday/01/1125/tokushu1.html).

Business@nifty, 7 December 2001 (http://business.nifty.com/news2/te/20011207te020.htm).

Fukushima News (http://headlines.yahoo.co.jp/hl?a=20020126-00000006-mai-l07).

"MIT to Make Nearly All Course Materials Available Free on the World Wide Web," (http:// web.mit.edu/newsoffice/nr/2001/ocw.html).

"The Actual Conditions of the Netherlands Model," (http://www.roumuya.net/zakkan/ zakkan13/dutch.html).

"The Chronology of Work-Sharing in Hyogo Prefecture," (http://web.pref.hyogo.jp/koyou/ worksharing/wshistr.htm).

Yomiuri Online, 14 April 2002 (http://www.yomiuri.co.jp/02/20020414ib01.htm).

"Young Applicants Swarming to Entrance Examination of SDF Assistant Reserve," Yomiuri Online, 14 April 2002 (http://www.yomiuri.co.jp/04/20020413i111.htm).

http://www.newtongym.ne.jp/_wyzup/businesssoft.htm

http://pcweb.mycom.co.jp/news/2001/12/07/22.html

http://www.cs.shinshu-u.ac.jp/Nyushi/sugsi/sugsipress.html

http://www.jitec.jp/index-e.html

http://www.jda.go.jp/j/defense/yobiji/yobiji.htm

http://www.kyoto-np.co.jp/kp/topics/2002mar/01/K20020301MKA2Z100000057.html

Index